NOTTINGHAM
26. SEPT, 2013

Stock picking for profit

Stock picking for profit

Simon Thompson

Published by Simon Thompson

Published by
Simon Thompson
PO Box 71272
London
SW11 9GW

First published in Great Britain in 2013

ISBN: 978-0-9576495-0-7

British Library Cataloguing-in-Publication Data
A catalogue record for this book is available from the British Library

10 9 8 7 6 5 4 3 2 1

Typeset in 9/13pt Stone Serif by Elaine Sharples (www.typesetter.org.uk)
Printed and bound by Ashford Colour Press Ltd, Gosport, Hants PO13 0FW

To my dearest wife Wendy – your invaluable support and efforts have made this book possible. I will be forever indebted.

Contents

Author's acknowledgements

I would like to extend a warm thank you to *Investors Chronicle* for the use of the magazine's extensive online archive, which has assisted me greatly in writing this book. In particular, I would like to offer my sincere gratitude to both Chris Dillow and Dominic Picarda for providing thought-provoking research into the areas of seasonal investing patterns and quantitative easing, respectively, and the implications for investing in equities. I have covered both subjects in great depth in this book. I would also like to thank Robert Ansted, statistics editor of *Investors Chronicle*, for his invaluable help and support. It has been greatly appreciated.

My thanks also to Credit Suisse Research Institute for enlightening me on the implications for inflation in a low growth, low return environment. In particular, I would like to extend by gratitude to Andrew Garthwaite, managing director of Credit Suisse global investment banking in London, and his global equity strategy team at the bank.

I am also indebted to the London Business School and emeritus professors Elroy Dimson, Paul Marsh and Mike Staunton, whose academic work into equity market returns has proved both thought-provoking and has major implications for asset allocation decisions.

I would also like to extend my gratitude to investment bank Numis for its great work into the analysis of the small-cap segment of the market, in collaboration with the London Business School. The bank's Numis Smaller Cap Index (NSCI) has proved invaluable in carrying out my analysis.

My thanks also to David Dreman, the founder, chairman and chief investment officer of US fund management group Dreman Value Management, for enlightening me on the merits of contrarian investing.

Finally, I would like to extend my gratitude to the three greatest investors of all-time: Warren Buffett, Benjamin Graham and Philip Fisher. The lessons I have learnt from these great men have provided the grounding to my understanding of financial analysis.

About the author

Simon Thompson has been Companies Editor at *Investors Chronicle*, the UK's leading investment magazine for private retail investors, for 12 years and has worked as a financial journalist for 15 years with the Financial Times Group in London. He has a BSc degree in banking and international finance from Cass Business School, City University, London.

Simon has an outstanding record of stock picking. His 2012 annual bargain shares portfolio in *Investors Chronicle* produced a total annual return of 31.9 per cent on an offer-to-bid basis, only marginally lagging behind the total return on the Fidelity UK Smaller Caps Fund, the best-performing small-cap fund of the 56 funds in this segment in the same period (*Investors Chronicle*, 'Bargain shares', 8 February 2013). Over the long run, Simon's record of stock picking by using this Benjamin Graham-inspired investment technique has stood the test of time and is in no small part down to the stellar performances of the undervalued small-cap shares he has consistently uncovered.

In the final quarter of 2012, Simon made no fewer than 24 recommendations on shares, indices and traded options in *Investors Chronicle*. These produced an average gain of 16.6 per cent on an offer-to-bid basis by mid-January 2013 (*Investors Chronicle*, 'Stock picking marvels', 16 January 2013).

The advice to magazine readers to buy the UK housebuilding sector at the start of 2013 also proved an astute call: the sector rallied over 20 per cent in the following three months. Simon also follows overseas financial markets. His portfolio of US stocks increased in value by 19.4 per cent on an offer-to-bid basis between the end of September 2012 and late January 2013, handsomely rewarding readers who followed his advice.

Simon is also the author of *Trading Secrets: 20 Hard and fast rules to help you beat the stock market*.

List of tables

Preface

When I decided to write *Stock Picking for Profit* my objective was simple: to write a book that could demonstrate how to successfully invest in equities by shrewdly picking shares.

The book had to be practical and needed to cover all the important areas of equity valuations. It also had to show how investment theory can be put into practice. To this end, I have provided no fewer than 32 case studies throughout the book to provide you with a step-by-step guide to explain the rationale for making these winning investments. I have also outlined the lessons to learn so that you too can implement the same techniques in your own stock picking.

The book includes important Warren Buffett and David Dreman-derived stock screens in the areas of value investing and contrarian investing, respectively. I have also given the 10 rules I use for screening my annual bargain shares (a Benjamin Graham-inspired stock screen) for *Investors Chronicle*. The aim here is for you to be able to do the same and enjoy the gains my portfolios have achieved over the years.

I believe *Stock Picking for Profit* is substantially a unique publication. There have been many academic titles published over the years, but my book differentiates itself in that the investment techniques highlighted have generated significant returns for the loyal readers of *Investors Chronicle* who have followed the share recommendations in my weekly columns.

By detailing the investment analysis that went into each recommendation, and showing how to carry out the analysis for yourself, *Stock Picking for Profit* is a book that offers the opportunity to learn from my knowledge of companies and financial markets. Read on and prosper!

Introduction

S uccessful stock picking involves understanding a variety of different elements, the most important of which is to be disciplined and to follow a set of rules that should help improve the chances of successs. That's why I have outlined my 20 golden rules of stock picking in the opening chapter.

It is also critical to understand accounting principles and valuation techniques. The easiest thing in the world for a company to do is to grow revenues and profits, which is why these are always the headline numbers at the top of press releases. It's not difficult, either, as all a company has to do is to suck in more capital to fund contract wins, the margin on which may not be that profitable at all. The net result is that a business can have rising revenues and profits, but at the same time be destroying shareholder value by generating lower and lower returns on its capital employed.

Thankfully, there are a number of investment techniques that can weed out those companies where businesses are actually low growth, so can only be expected to generate low long-term returns as a consequence, setting them apart from those whose prospects are far brighter.

A good starting point is to analyse a company's cash flow and cash generation, which I have done in Chapter 2. You can then take this a stage further and consider how cash on the balance sheet impacts valuations. In detailed case studies I show how companies trading on relatively full looking earnings multiples can offer compelling investment opportunities, simply by using certain well-tried valuation techniques.

Clearly, not all companies are cash-rich and I have dedicated a whole chapter to balance sheet strength and debt. That's because some of the most spectacular gains I have racked up on my stock picks have been made from shares priced on large discounts to book value. However, it's important to differentiate between companies that are being undervalued by the market even though their finances are sound, and those where the financial risk is far greater, and so warrant a lower rating than peers whose finances are in better shape. In three case studies in Chapter 3, I highlight the importance of debt structures on valuations and how to uncover undervalued companies.

Capital returns form a major part of shareholders' investment returns. There are several ways companies can do this. Fortunately it's possible to make money from all of them. Share buy-backs, tender offers and special dividends are the three I focus on most. In chapter 4, I outline how investors can exploit these capital returns.

It is fair to say that my investment style is that of a classic value investor. In particular, I look for companies being valued well below net asset value or where the sum-of-the-parts valuation reveals hidden value. In chapter 5, I highlight the key points to look out for to help you pick out the winners from the losers.

Another benefit of my balance-sheet-based approach to stock picking is that it uncovers investment opportunities that are also potential bid targets. One method of seeking out likely bid targets is to focus on good-quality companies with strong balance sheets offering potential for an earnings recovery, but where the assets are being modestly priced relative to their book value. Even if this is the case, a takeover is unlikely to happen unless the majority shareholders can be persuaded to part with their paper and there is a willing buyer. In Chapter 6, I reveal what to look for in bid targets and show how to play the merger arbitrage game profitably.

Ultimately, it doesn't matter how lowly a company is valued, you need a spark to ignite the share price to re-rate. The one most likely is the most obvious: an improvement in the trading performance. In Chapter 7, I outline the important signals to look for to identify recovery plays. Moreover, when a company's operational performance starts to gain momentum, it pays to monitor key indicators. That's because gains can be made by riding on the coat-tails of a company in an upgrade cycle, as revealed in Chapter 8.

Sometimes director buying can be a great buy signal, especially in recovery plays. But director share dealing in small-caps and the lower end of the mid-cap segment of the market is always worth investigating. That's because it can be an amber signal that trading prospects are far better than outside investors think. When a number of directors are all buying at the same time the message is clear: the board believes that the company is being undervalued and aims to exploit this in a big way. In Chapter 9, I reveal how to spot the gems by following the lead of the insiders.

As part of my investment analysis, I always have a close look at technical indicators. A company may tick all the right boxes, but if the chart is telling you something different then this should raise alarm bells. So, in order to identify shares that have a positive set-up on their charts, and to avoid the ones where the technical set-up is unfavourable, I use a number of tried and tested systems to determine whether investing in a company is warranted. In Chapter 10, I highlight the ones that have consistently uncovered great buying opportunities.

It is also important to be aware of the risk embedded in a company's valuation, as any two companies will have a different risk profile. The aim is to maximise the return available by taking as little risk as possible. In Chapter 11, I outline the 16 different risk assessments I carry out on every company I analyse to get a picture of the level of investment risk.

A company may appear undervalued based on fundamental investment analysis, and the chart set-up may be relatively positive, but investing in the wrong sector at the wrong time of the year is like running up a down escalator. To avoid this, it's best to know which segments of the market perform best and at which points of the year as I highlight in Chapter 12.

I have been an avid follower of the small-cap and micro-cap segment of the stock market over the years and no more so when it comes to my stock recommendations for *Investors Chronicle*. This is partly because these companies are under-researched by analysts, and below the radar of fund managers, so offer greater potential to uncover anomalous valuations. It's only sensible to target the parts of the market where you expect the best returns to be made.

Our history books also reveal some telling long-term trends from small-cap investing as I explain in Chapter 13. For instance, I highlight how to enhance portfolio performance by targeting small-cap companies trading on low price-to-book-value ratios and offering above-average dividend yields. It is possible to take this one stage further by introducing additional selection criteria to narrow down the shortlist of potential investment candidates. In Chapter 14, I show how to do this by focusing on contrarian investment strategies and using certain stock screening techniques.

I also use stock screening for my annual bargain shares portfolios in *Investors Chronicle*. This idea is very simple: to invest in companies where the true worth of the assets are not reflected in the share price, usually for some temporary reason, but where we can reasonably expect them to be reassessed in due course. In Chapter 15, I reveal the systems I employ to uncover these undervalued companies and ones that have stood the test of time.

I set some fairly stringent rules in my stock selection process to maximise the chances of making the greatest returns by taking the least amount of risk. These rules help me avoid the pitfalls of selecting shares where the odds of generating a positive return are less than favourable for the risk being taken. In Chapter 16, I outline risk management techniques to follow in order to maximise gains and minimise losses.

In recent years, those gains have largely been driven by the unconventional monetary policy of the world's central banks, otherwise known as 'quantitative easing' (QE). If you ever doubted the power of the US Federal Reserve (Fed), the past four years have been a textbook case of how the world's leading central bank continues to have a massive influence on financial markets. It therefore pays to know where to invest during new rounds of QE as I reveal in Chapter 17.

Assuming these QE programmes work, this will raise consumption and drive economies back into growth. But when that happens it is only reasonable to assume that inflation will rise too. This has obvious implications for equity markets since some sectors do well during periods of rising inflation and some should be avoided at all costs. Fortunately, I have a good idea how equities are likely to behave in such an environment, as I highlight in Chapter 18.

The world's greatest investor, Warren Buffett, whose Berkshire Hathaway investment vehicle has proved itself to be the most successful investment company of all-time, undoubtedly does too. In Chapter 19, I reveal the important lessons I have learned from the sage of Omaha and how I use them in my investment analysis.

Finally, in Chapter 20, I reveal the advice I would offer any reader to achieve profitable outcomes. True, past success in stock picking is no guarantee of the same in the future, so don't expect to have a profitable outcome every time you apply the investment techniques outlined in this book. However, what these techniques should do is to shift the odds in your favour and improve the chances of success as a stock picker in the long run.

The 20 golden rules to profitable stock picking

I f there is one thing I have learned from following financial markets for a quarter of a century, it is that relying purely on company accounts and analysts' research is simply not enough to find profitable investment opportunities. There are a multitude of other factors that need to be considered and, in this chapter, I highlight the 20 investment rules that have aided my success in stock picking over the years.

1. Heed the bigger picture

You should always consider the bigger macroeconomic picture and how developments in other markets are impacting investment trends. For instance, between November 2008 and April 2013 the actions of the world's leading central banks in the US, UK, Europe and more recently, Japan, have had a great influence in determining the direction of equity markets.

As I will illustrate in later chapters, the quantitative easing programmes (money printing) carried out by the world's most important central bank, the US Federal Reserve, have been a major driver of stock market performances across the globe. This has a major bearing on which sectors investors should focus on within these markets while unconventional monetary policies are being adopted.

For instance, in the summer of 2012, the European Central Bank finally agreed to employ its massive balance sheet to purchase government bonds from the southern Mediterranean block of countries to stop the region's debt contagion spreading any further. This policy decision led to a sharp fall in secondary market sovereign bond yields for both Italy and Spain. It also meant that a significant amount of risk embedded in equity market valuations was removed at a stroke, which in turn fuelled a sharp rally in all western stock markets.

2. Go global

Investing in international markets has never been easier. With the benefit of low-cost online share dealing, it is possible for any retail investor to capitalise on overseas investment opportunities that were once only available to large institutional funds.

For instance, some of the biggest and most profitable companies in the world, including smartphone and tablet maker Apple and online search engine Google, have produced scintillating earnings growth in the past decade, driven by an insatiable appetite for technology from consumers across the globe. At a click of a mouse, investors have been able to ride on the coat-tails of the staggering share price gains enjoyed by shareholders in these companies.

A key investment decision to make is how much of your capital (financial and human) you are willing to allocate to sourcing these international opportunities.

3. Understand correlations and trends

Uncovering correlations in the way sectors perform, and markets in general, can be a great way of boosting financial returns and reducing risk at the same time. But never buy blind. Just because a correlation has held in the past, it doesn't mean to say that it will always. The fundamental case for investing has to be strong, too.

4. Inflation

It's not just the level of inflation that has an impact on asset allocation decisions and the likely returns investors can expect from equities and bonds. Equally as important is the future expectation of inflation, as this has a major bearing on real bond yields (nominal bond yields adjusted for inflation). And it is the combination of the level and direction of real bond yields, future expectation of inflation, and the inflation rate itself which determine the sectors likely to perform well or badly. I will discuss this issue in great detail in chapter 18.

5. Monitor earnings cycles

It is important to identify whether analyst expectations are achievable, be it for a market, sector or company. It is far harder for a market to rally in the face of an earnings downgrade cycle when analyst earnings estimates are being reined back and investor sentiment is being dampened.

Also, when an earnings cycle peaks for a company, and is coupled with a peak valuation, then this can be a good signal that the time is rapidly approaching to bank gains.

6. Assess risk

It is a good discipline to carry out a risk assessment on any potential investment. This focuses the mind on the nature of the risks being taken on and whether the potential returns are great enough to warrant an investment. In order to do this, I carry out 16 different risk assessments on every company I analyse to get a picture of the level of risk. A company has to pass at least 10 of these tests to make it onto my shortlist.

7. Relative valuations are important

Equity returns are also determined by relative valuations both at a market level and on a sector basis. This is why the quantitative easing programmes between November 2008 and April 2013 have led to such dramatic movements in a number of asset classes and none more so than in equity markets. That's because central banks have been attempting (successfully) to alter how investors value equities relative to fixed income.

By actively driving up the value of bonds that exist in many investors' portfolios it encourages them to rebalance their assets more towards equities to maintain current allocations. Central bankers have also been attempting to incentivise fund flows into the equity market, which boosts household wealth and makes consumers who hold shares feel better off. In turn, this has a major impact on which sectors perform best in this type of environment, a subject I will discuss in chapter 17.

8. Size matters

I have a keen interest in the small-cap and micro-cap segment of the market. This is for a very good reason: size really does matter. In fact, research from the Credit Suisse Research Institute in collaboration with the London Business School shows that, since 1955, the UK equity market has produced an annualised return of 12.4 per cent. However, UK small-caps have performed even better, rising by an average of 15.3 per cent a year based on the performance of the RBS HSGC index, which measures the performance of the lowest tenth of the main UK equity market by market value. And micro-caps have done even better, producing an average annualised return of 18.1 per cent.

9. Value premium matters

My focus on value stocks is not without foundation either. According to research carried out by professors Elroy Dimson, Paul Marsh and Mike Staunton of the London Business School, UK listed companies with a high book-to-market value (value stocks) have produced an annualised return of 16.6 per cent since 1955, whereas those with a low book-to-market value (growth stocks) produced an annualised return of 10.4 per cent in the same period. This explains why the value segment of the market accounts for the majority of my share recommendations for *Investors Chronicle*.

10. Dividends pay

Dividends are crucial in generating long-term portfolio returns, so it pays to understand the income premium. In the UK, the income premium between the highest yielders in the market and the lowest yielders is 3 percentage points, according to research from the London Business School. This may not sound much, but the differences are marked when compounded over time.

In fact, a high-yielding portfolio generating an annualised 10.9 per cent total return (figures calculated since 1900 on the UK stock market) would be worth over 50 per cent more than a low-yielding portfolio (returning 7.8 per cent a year) within only 15 years. These returns factor in the reinvestment of dividends.

11. Recycling cash

Companies with net cash positions or low balance sheet gearing, and an improving operational performance, can recycle cash flow into value-added acquisitions to boost profits. This also creates an attractive investment proposition whereby some of the profits earned by acquired businesses can then be recycled as dividend income to shareholders. This underpins a progressive dividend policy.

12. Avoid companies with poor cash conversion

Companies reporting rising profits and deteriorating cash flow is seriously not good news. It's even worse if the profit growth is being accompanied by rising debt levels as this can indicate that the business is sucking in increasing amounts of capital to fund growth and is probably generating pretty low returns, too. It also raises questions about how profitable the business really is if the cash position is worsening markedly.

13. Understand debt

The biggest corporate failures in the past few decades have all been companies that have been saddled with unsustainable debt levels and weak cash generation. Refinancing is the ticking time bomb for many companies, especially in tighter credit environments. Understanding how businesses finance their operations and the robustness of their cash flow is critical in assessing any potential investment.

14. Be conservative with discounted cash flow models

The problem with discounted cash flow (DCF) models is that valuing a company based on its future cash flow generation is wrought with difficulties, as the calculation is dependent on several variables, of which many are subjective. In fact, tweak assumptions of a company's future growth rates; the discount rate applied to value future cash flow; and the company's average weighted cost of capital; and you will come up with a totally different valuation for any company. I therefore take a conservative approach to DCF-derived valuations from analysts.

15. Profit from new listings

In bull markets, the success or failure of a new listing has as much to do with the attraction of the valuation being offered to new investors relative to that of peers, as investor sentiment itself. Shares rarely peak out at fair value. So if the company has been keenly priced to leave enough upside on the table for new investors, then they are likely to take the hint and show an appetite in the secondary market.

For instance, shares in housebuilder Crest Nicholson soared 40 per cent within two months of listing on the main board of the London stock market in early 2013. It was not an isolated example, either, as shares in insurer Direct Line rose almost 30 per cent above the company's float price within three months of its float in mid-October 2012. These share price gains, both of which were considerably more than the return from the FTSE 100 and FTSE 250 indices in the same periods, were also driven by technical buying from index-tracking funds in the secondary market. Direct Line went straight into the FTSE 250 and Crest Nicholson is expected to take its place in the same index by mid-2013.

It's therefore worth considering the potential for technical buying to buoy share prices of newly listed companies in the secondary market.

16. Find out when lock-in periods end

Major shareholders and directors can be prevented from selling shares directly after a flotation or when a company pays for an acquisition in shares. Therefore, it is worth finding out when lock-ins expire as this can lead to a technical stock overhang if there is a persistent seller in the market.

This is one reason why shares in the social networking website Facebook, the largest internet-related international public offering (IPO) ever, performed so poorly on Nasdaq in 2012. Investors were clearly wary of the large amounts of stock that could come onto the market from existing shareholders. A heady earnings multiple didn't help the shares in the aftermarket either.

17. Follow the charts

Charting or technical analysis has as many sceptics as converts. No matter which side of the fence you sit on, charts are incredibly useful in highlighting trends based on historic price data. I would never contemplate recommending any investment without first carrying out extensive technical analysis. Moreover, so many investors use technical analysis as part of their investment decision process that it would be foolish not to find out what the charts are indicating prior to making your decision.

18. Liquidity counts

Always monitor the share price moves of a company and how sensitive they are to changes in daily trading volume. This is important as prices of some companies can spike on very low trading volumes due to low free floats and the substantial shareholdings of a few investors, which limit the number of shares that can be readily traded. While this can create accentuated price moves to the upside on good newsflow, as soon as investors head for the exit, the downside ride can be equally hair-raising.

19. Seasonal investing trends

Investing at the wrong time of year in the wrong sector is a sure-fire way of making sub-standard returns. So it pays to be aware of which trends work best at certain points of the year. Otherwise, you could find yourself running up a down escalator while other investors are looking down on you from several floors up, having capitalised on the profitable market trends that have a habit of repeating themselves again and again.

20. Monitor directors' dealings

Directors are fully entitled to reap the benefits of their labour, and if share options are a part of the package, it is only fair they be allowed to take advantage and sell down holdings at some point. Although share dealing on a limited scale can be largely ignored, alarm bells should start ringing when several directors start selling down a sizeable chunk of their stakes. Equally, when a director is a persistent buyer in the market, making significant share purchases, this can be a tell-tale sign that the insiders know something worth investigating.

chapter

2

Cash is king

M any investors only focus on a few headline figures when looking at company announcements and PR companies make it easy to fall into this trap by portraying their clients' performance in the best possible light. However, the easiest thing in the world for a company to do is to grow revenues and profits, which is why these are nearly always the headline numbers at the top of any press release.

It's not difficult either, as all a company has to do is to suck in more capital to fund contract wins, although the margins on these may not be that profitable at all. The net result is that a business can have rising revenues and profits, but at the same time be destroying shareholder value by generating lower and lower returns on its capital employed.

Another way to boost profits is through acquisitions, but ultimately you have to ask whether or not scaling up a business is warranted. To do this, you have to decide whether the net profits generated from the combined operation justifies the additional capital employed in the merged entity.

Thankfully, there are a number of investment techniques you can use to weed out the companies whose businesses are actually low growth, and so can only be expected to generate low long-term returns, as opposed to those whose prospects are far brighter. One starting point is to analyse a company's cash flow and cash generation.

Cash profits

One method I use in my financial analysis is to calculate the cash profits which, in a company's accounts, is shown as earnings before interest, taxation, depreciation and amortisation (Ebitda). This can be worked out by adding back depreciation and amortisation charges to the reported operating profits (Ebit). Importantly, depreciation and amortisation are both non-cash charges, so by adding them back, it gives a more accurate idea of the cash profitability of a business.

I then work out the company's enterprise value, which is the sum of its market value and net borrowing. Alternatively, for a company with a cash-rich balance sheet, enterprise value is its market value less net cash. The next step is to compare the ratio of a company's enterprise value (EV) to Ebitda, which in some analyst notes will be referred to as EV/Ebitda.

The benefit of using this ratio to analyse individual companies, or to make comparisons across a sector, is that it removes the distortions that result from different companies carrying varying levels of debt. It also makes it quite easy to see the underlying performance of a company that has gone on an acquisition spree and so boosted the Ebitda line, but has also increased its EV by either issuing new shares to finance the acquisitions or by borrowing to do so.

---

case study 1

How capital structures affect valuations

To illustrate how different capital structures impact on how companies are valued by investors, consider a company that has no debt on its balance sheet, but decides to gear up and borrow from banks in order to pay back a chunk of capital to shareholders.

The company will still make the same cash profits after paying back capital to shareholders as it did before, and will still have the same number of shares in issue. So if the share price falls by the same amount as the one-off dividend per share, it is paying to shareholders by using the extra capital borrowed, then the EV line doesn't change at all. That's because the reduction in the market value following the dividend payment is exactly the same as the increase in debt. And clearly the Ebitda line doesn't change either, so the ratio remains the same.

However, the additional interest payments on the debt taken on by the company to make the one-off dividend payment depresses reported profits and means that net profits per share, or EPS, fall. And because the company is carrying more debt on the balance sheet investors may decide that it carries more risk and are prepared to pay slightly less for those earnings.

For example, if the company has a share price of 100p and is making **EPS** of 10p a year, then its PE ratio is 10 before making a capital return. Let's say that it returns 20p a share to shareholders through a dividend, having borrowed this money from its banks, the cost of which is 1p a share net of tax in annual finance charges. So after the capital return, the company is carrying net debt of 20p a share, has a share price of 80p and now makes EPS of 9p. But its **PE** ratio is now 9 rather than 10 to reflect the extra debt on the balance sheet.

This is why it is wrong to think that a company is undervalued because it has a lower PE ratio than another company in the same sector with the same characteristics, without taking the different capital structures into account.

Key lesson to learn:

■ **Enterprise value to cash profit ratio.** This ratio is important in assessing the cash generation of a company in relation to the amount of equity and debt employed and irons out the distortions in the PE ratio which lead to 'value traps'. This is where highly indebted companies with low PE ratios appear undervalued compared with cash-rich or lowly geared companies with higher PE ratios. These are in fact being fairly valued once you take into account the different capital structure.

---

case study 2

Adjusting for cash profits

The EV/Ebitda multiple can be used to uncover undervalued companies that carry high cash balances but earn very little in the way of interest income. These companies may look highly rated on a simple earnings multiple using reported EPS when, in fact, they offer great value.

A good example of this is clothing retailer Moss Bros, which I analysed in great depth in the *Investors Chronicle* in early 2012 following the sale of the company's Hugo Boss franchise (*Investors Chronicle*, 'Dressed for success', 20 February 2012). This left the company's balance sheet in a cash-rich position.

Plan for growth

Moss Bros's management had a plan to upgrade 90 stores over a three- to five-year period at a cost of around £11m, and to invest heavily in a new internet offering. This meant there was a growth story to get sales moving again, especially as the results of trial refurbishments showed that underlying sales got an immediate lift and the capital outlay of between £40,000 and £240,000 per store was recouped in a reasonable time frame. Combined with the relaunch of the retailer's own brands and streamlining those of third-parties, it was reasonable to assume that both revenues and margins would get a boost.

Analyse cash generation

On further inspection, I realised just how cash-generative Moss Bros's underlying business is, so much so that the company's cash pile rose by £2.4m to £25.7m in the financial year ending January 2013. That increase in net cash was after Moss Bros made capital investments of £5.5m in the 12-month period, so the expenditure in store refits was entirely funded from cash flow.

To illustrate this, I carry out a simple calculation by adding back the company's £4.55m depreciation charge and £0.6m amortisation charge (both non-cash) to the annual operating profits of £2.73m. This produces Ebitda, or cash profits, of £7.9m. This is not only significantly higher than the company's capital expenditure of £5.5m, but means that the £5.1m non-cash charge for depreciation and amortisation covered almost all of the capital spend, leaving enough cash over to swell the cash pile even further.

Adjust for cash pile

So although Moss Bros's shares may appear ridiculously rated on 32 times reported post-tax earnings per share (EPS), it is misleading to value the company on this basis. That's because, once you strip out the £25.7m cash pile from the market value of £65m, the company's enterprise value of £39m is only five times historic cash profits before tax of £7.9m. Moreover, investment in refurbishments has created a virtuous circle where incremental profits can be recycled into new refits, which in turn boost profits. In fact, analysts expect cash profits to rise by a further £500,000 to £8.4m in the financial year to January 2014.

It is this enviable cash generation, coupled with a recovery and growth story, that explains why the shares soared by 80 per cent in the 12 months after I highlighted the investment potential in the *Investors Chronicle.*

Key lessons to learn:

■ **Cash generation**. Cash-rich companies with high PE ratios may appear overvalued when in fact they are attractively priced once you strip out the low-yielding cash pile.

■ **Net cash position mitigates risk**. Companies with low borrowings or a net cash position can significantly reduce investment risk because investors focus more on the operational performance and ability of management to grow cash flow and profits and far less on financial risk.

■ **Operating cash flow.** If non-cash charges (which have the impact of lowering reported operating and pre-tax profits in the accounts), exceed capital expenditure then companies can maintain investment in the business and still generate excess cash flow for the benefit of shareholders.

■ **Creating a virtuous circle.** Assuming the returns made by recycling internal cash flow back into the business exceed the cost of capital, then recycling cash flow will create shareholder value. In the case of Moss Bros, the company's cash pile is low yielding in the current low-interest-rate environment, so given the cash payback on invested capital in new stores is relatively short at 24 months, the company is creating value for all shareholders by recycling cash in this way.

---

case study 3

Adjusted earnings multiples

As highlighted by Moss Bros, valuing companies on a standard PE multiple can give a completely misleading view of the value in the underlying business when there are substantial cash holdings on the balance sheet. In fact, given the low-interest-rate environment, a company's PE ratio may appear high when, in effect, it is relatively modest when you adjust for these cash holdings.

A great example of this is one of my best share recommendations over the past couple of years, Netcall, a small-cap company offering software to make telephone call-handling more efficient (*Investors Chronicle*, 'Queuebusters', 17 January 2011). Like many software companies, Netcall retains a decent amount of net cash on its balance sheet, which funds working capital and provides clients with the reassurance that the company is in a strong enough financial position to be able to service contracts. At the end of December 2012, the company had net funds of £8.2m, or around 20 per cent of its market value of £44m, and no debt.

Factoring in the net cash position

Netcall's shares trebled in value from 13p to 39.5p since the start of 2011 when I first highlighted the investment potential of the company in the *Investors Chronicle*. By April 2013, they were trading on 19.5 times historic EPS of 2p. However, if you strip out net cash of 7p a share from the company's share price, adjust the EPS figure for loss of investment income and then recalculate the PE ratio, you get a far more accurate idea of the earnings multiple, which is actually nearer 16 'net of cash'.

Moreover, with analysts expecting the company's earnings per share to rise by 15 per cent from 2p to 2.3p for the 12 months to end-June 2013, then the forward PE ratio on a 'net of cash' basis is actually 14.

Recycling cash flow

This only tells part of the story because, with cash generation strong and the cash pile rising, Netcall is able to redeploy some of the burgeoning cash pile into making bolt-on acquisitions, which add value to the business by generating cross-selling opportunities across its existing operations. This robust cash generation also has the added benefit of enabling Netcall's board to adopt a progressive dividend policy.

As a result, shareholders are benefiting from a growing income stream, and a business generating increasing profits. It's hardly surprising that the shares have surged because as long as Netcall is being valued by investors on an adjusted 'net of cash' PE ratio of around 14, to reflect the double-digit annual earnings growth it is generating, then the rising EPS will lead to a rising share price to maintain the PE ratio.

Key lessons to learn:

■ **Adjusted earnings multiples**. Companies in certain sectors are more likely to carry net cash positions on the balance sheet as this reassures their customers that the companies will be around to fulfil contracts, some of which may be multi-year agreements. So it is imperative to factor in the cash position when trying to make peer group comparisons.

■ **Recycling cash**. Companies with net cash positions and reporting an improving operational performance can recycle cash flow into value-added acquisitions. This boosts profits for the company and creates a virtuous circle whereby some of the operating profits made by acquired businesses can then be recycled into dividends to shareholders, which underpins a more progressive dividend policy.

case study 4

Special dividends

The investment technique of adjusting valuations for cash on the balance sheet has a habit of throwing up some bargain basement investment opportunities, such as Indigovision, a pioneer in internet protocol network-based security surveillance systems.

When I recommended buying the shares (*Investors Chronicle*, 'Bargain shares', 10 February 2012), analysts were predicting that the company's pre-tax profits would more than double from £1.2m to £2.7m in the 12 months to end-July 2012. On this basis, EPS was forecast to more than treble to 25.8p, up from 8.4p in 2011. This boost to profits reflected the benefits of a lower cost base following restructuring and the fact that operating margins had fallen to unacceptably low levels in the previous financial year and were set to recover. So with the share price around 325p, the company was being valued on a reasonable 13 times forward earnings if management could deliver on those forecasts.

There was value on the balance sheet as Indigovision was sitting on almost 100p a share of net cash. Strip this out, and the forward PE ratio fell from a reasonable 13 times earnings estimates to a bargain basement 8.7 times earnings net of cash. By spotting the company had a cash-rich balance sheet and was set to deliver a huge increase in profits literally paid dividends when Indigovision released bumper results in September 2012. The announcement included a hefty 75p-a-share payout to shareholders. This sparked a 70 per cent rerating of the shares as the value on offer became abundantly apparent to a wider investor audience.

Key lessons to learn:

■ **Capital returns**. Adjusting a company's PE ratio for its net cash position gives a truer reflection of the earnings multiple.

■ **Cash pile**. When a company's cash pile is rising, and there is excess capital on its balance sheet, the board is far more likely to return this to shareholders. When this happens, investors reassess the investment case.

■ **Special dividends.** Companies that have a habit of paying out special dividends are far more likely to do so again when the payout is under-pinned by a strong cash flow performance.

3

Balance sheet strength and debt

S ome of the most spectacular gains I have racked up on my stock picks have been made from companies valued on large discounts to **net asset value (NAV)** even though they have substantial asset backing. However, it is important to differentiate between companies that are being undervalued by the market even though their finances are sound, and those where the financial risk is far greater and so warrant a lower rating than peers whose finances are in better shape.

Debt levels can be a dead weight for a share price as investors naturally become more cautious if borrowings are too high in relation to assets held and operating cash flow generated. It's not difficult to understand why this is the case, since investment risk rises as a company's debt increases and not just default risk. That's because the ability of a company to invest in the business is restricted if debt levels, and interest payments on those borrowings are too high, since finance charges will eat up a much higher proportion of cash flow.

High debt levels also undermine the scope of the board to adopt a more progressive dividend policy, because the cash that would otherwise be used to raise the payout is being paid out to fund borrowings instead. And since dividends account for a large chunk of the total return long-term investors expect from holding shares, then companies offering lower dividend growth rates are likely to be given relatively lower ratings.

It's therefore best to avoid highly geared companies for the simple fact that it's one thing taking on operational risk, but completely another exposing your investment capital to the financial risk of a company being unable to service its borrowings at the same time. It's for this reason that I try to target companies sitting on net cash, or modest levels of debt, and have the asset backing to mitigate financial risk.

Understanding debt

It is important to understand how a company is financing its operations and whether there are any issues with its credit lines. This is even more important for small and medium-sized companies in difficult credit environments when availability of finance is more restrictive. Lenders are also in a strong position to demand even more restrictive covenants on the debt when it comes up for refinancing.

As a result, when you carry out your investment analysis it is imperative to check the maturity dates and terms of credit lines in the notes to a company's accounts to ascertain whether refinancing is going to be an issue. That's another reason to avoid highly geared companies as lenders can easily force companies to reduce their debt levels on refinancing. When this happens, the only option left is for the board to go cap in hand to shareholders to tap them for the extra capital needed to repay lenders. Alternatively, an outside investor could be brought in, but given the weak bargaining position, existing shareholders would face significant dilution of their holdings in the company.

It is no coincidence that some of the highest profile corporate failures in 2012 and 2013 – HMV, JJB Sports and Clinton Cards – were carrying substantial and unsustainable levels of debt when their lenders pulled the plug, wiping out shareholders in the process.

Understanding how a company finances itself can pay bumper returns too, as highlighted by the case of Aim-traded property developer Terrace Hill.

case study 5

De-gearing and reducing investment risk

I selected shares in Terrace Hill, a small-cap property developer and investor, as one of my top 10 value shares for 2013 (*Investors Chronicle*, 'Bargain shares for 2013', 8 February 2013).

At the time, the shares were trading a hefty 38 per cent below net asset value, which partly reflected the fact that debt maturity on the company's loans was short-dated and had an average maturity of only 12.5 months. However, I didn't expect there to be any refinancing issues since the loan-to-value ratio on the company's properties was less than 50 per cent and balance sheet gearing was relatively modest at just over 50 per cent. Terrace Hill also had a major shareholder, chairman Robert Adair, who owns 62.87 per cent of the issued share capital and has a vested interest in making sure that his company is able to refinance its debts.

Within weeks the company had announced two major disposals, including the sale of 95 per cent of its wholly owned residential property assets, as part of a strategic move to focus its activities more on developing food stores for supermarkets. Factoring in the net proceeds from the disposals, net borrowings were slashed from £47.2m at the September 2012 financial year-end to only £20.2m by February 2013. In turn, this reduced balance sheet gearing to only 34.6 per cent of shareholders' funds of £58.4m. Further debt reductions were on the cards because Terrace Hill had started a programme of sales to owner-occupiers for the remainder of the group's residential portfolio, which had a book value of £5.5m.

In the circumstances, it's hardly surprising that the company's share price rocketed over 25 per cent in a matter of weeks once the refinancing risk embedded in the share price discount to net asset value had been removed. In light of these large disposals (sold at book value), other investors who had shied away from the company's shares previously were now far more likely to find the investment case attractive given the much reduced financial risk.

Key lessons to learn:

- **Assess financial risk.** A good practice when carrying out investment analysis is to assess the financial risk embedded in a company's current valuation and ascertain how this risk would change if the company made a major disposal and slashed borrowings.

- **Gearing levels.** As a rule, try to avoid companies with balance sheet gearing levels above 80 per cent as the financial risk embedded in the valuations is likely to rise sharply above this level.

- **Operational cash flow.** Assess whether cash flow is strong and sustainable enough to comfortably pay down the annual interest bill on borrowings and whether there is enough cash left over to actually pay down debt. Avoid companies where interest cover is so tight that there is no room for manoeuvre. As a rule of thumb, avoid companies where the ratio of operating profit to net interest payments is below two to mitigate financial risk.

Convertible debt

Investors should pay particular attention to the small print when a company intends to raise funds through a convertible bond issue. Unless the conversion terms are capped, there is a huge incentive for convertible bondholders to drive down a company's share price (by short-selling the shares) in order to maximise the number of shares issued to them on conversion. In a bear market, this can accentuate downward pressure on a company's share price and lead to a significant dilution for existing shareholders due to the technical stock overhang.

Generally, conversion of the debt into equity is calculated at the average of the lowest closing share price over a specified period prior to the day of conversion. If there is a cap on the lowest conversion price, or a collar on the maximum number of shares that can be issued under the terms of the bonds, then this will create a share price floor below which there is no incentive for bondholders to drive down the shares any further. When the market is rising, this is less of a problem. However, in bear markets the interests of equity shareholders and convertible bondholders are clearly not aligned – unless there are limits placed on the conversion terms to dissuade bondholders from short-selling, which is rarely the case.

It's therefore imperative to understand the terms of the convertible bonds or loan notes to determine whether the interests of bondholders and shareholders are aligned. The case of Indian power developer Greenko is a good example.

---

case study 6

Understanding conversion terms

When Greenko, the Indian developer, owner and operator of clean energy projects, announced in March 2013 a proposed £100m investment in its subsidiary by an affiliate of the Government of Singapore Investment Corporation (GIC), one of the world's leading sovereign wealth funds, shares in the company got an immediate lift. It was easy to see why, because the terms of the deal struck were skewed in favour of the company's shareholders and also enabled Greenko to ramp up the construction of its substantial power portfolio and take advantage of the attractive power opportunities in India.

The sovereign wealth fund was clearly taken by the investment case because the £100m invested converts on a one-for-one basis into ordinary shares in Greenko at a price of 260p per share, subject to final adjustment between 1 July 2015 and 30 June 2017. That means the issue of 38.26m shares, or the equivalent of 19.5 per cent of Greenko's enlarged share capital on a fully diluted basis. Given Greenko's share price was only 118p prior to the announcement, this highlighted the significant potential upside in the value of the clean energy projects GIC was investing in.

The main point to note here is that the conversion price has been set well above the current share price, so the interests of existing shareholders and the new investors are aligned.

Key lessons to learn:

- **Conversion terms.** The notes to a company's accounts will explain the conversion terms of loan notes or convertible debt into equity. Always assess whether there is enough headroom between the conversion price of the debt and the current share price to enable convertible bondholders to convert their debt without adversely affecting the company's share price.

■ **Shareholder base.** If convertible bondholders have outright control of a company on conversion of their debt into equity then, in effect, the company is not being controlled by existing shareholders, but by debt holders. This can have negative implications for the value ascribed to the company's equity by other investors.

■ **Assess return on capital.** Since the cost of equity is far higher than the cost of debt for the majority of companies, it is paramount to assess whether the funds raised by issuing the convertible debt can actually generate a return on invested capital above the company's cost of capital.

Changing capital structures

It is always important to assess whether the capital structure in place is suitable for the type of business. For instance, property and utility companies have much higher debt levels in relation to their net assets than other companies since they have stable income streams which can service borrowings. It is quite common for gearing ratios to be above 100 per cent without putting the interests of shareholders at risk.

But even when a company's board feels its current borrowing levels are too high, if the reason for issuing new equity in order to pay down the debt is sound then this can have a positive impact on the shares. This means existing shareholders benefit from lower investment risk due to a reduction in the financial risk the shares carry. They can also enjoy a share price rerating as a consequence.

To show how this works in practice, consider the case of marketing services provider Communisis, a company for which I first highlighted the investment case in early 2012 (*Investors Chronicle*, 'A small-cap trading play', 12 February 2012).

case study 7

Equity fundraisings and debt

Following a major cost-cutting and site consolidation programme, by the end of 2011 five of the Communisis' 14 sites had been closed and around £4m cut from the annual cost base at a one-off cash cost of £2m. The plan was to use half of the saving to fund a move up into higher-margin data, digital and creative services to drive revenues ahead.

Management was also being strict with existing contracts in order to boost overall profitability. It could afford to, because new contract wins were more than offsetting lost business, including major deals with global consumer goods giant Procter & Gamble and Nationwide Building Society. This meant that the combination of higher-margin sales and a lower cost base were driving profits up sharply.

Moreover, borrowings of £25.9m equated to a modest 19 per cent of net assets, and having refinanced credit lines in 2011, the company's bank facilities were secured for another two-and-a-half years. Dividend cover was comfortable too – over two-and-a-half times covered by operating profits in 2011. For a company generating double-digit earnings growth there was obvious value in the shares, rated on a miserly 5.5 times earnings estimates for the 2012 financial year and offering a prospective yield of over 5 per cent.

Fundraising announced

At the start of 2013, the recovery was bang on track and investors had started to acknowledge this; the share price had risen by over 50 per cent. It was therefore with great interest that I noted the company announced an equity fundraising. The proceeds were to be used in three main areas of the business: investment in new contracts (around £6m of the £18.9m net proceeds); to fund previously announced restructuring costs of £1.4m; and to make small acquisitions and fund working capital (around £11.5m).

This looked a sensible use of the funds as Communisis had been winning significant (and profitable) long-term new contracts in the first three months of 2013, including further long-term agreements with BT and Nationwide Building Society. In fact, around 70 per cent of 2013 revenues were expected to come from multi-year contracts. This is good for profits, and underpins analyst profit estimates, but it meant Communisis needed to invest in working capital and capital expenditure to fulfil new contract wins. Restructuring the direct mail operations and consolidation of facilities made strategic sense, as this would make the business more efficient, reduce overheads and boost profitability.

True, the company only had net borrowings of £21m at the end of December 2012, which equated to 16 per cent of shareholders' funds of £128m, so the balance sheet was hardly stretched. Communisis was also trading well within its new credit facility of £55m. But it still made sense to keep borrowings as low as possible rather than run up higher debt levels to fund the increased working capital and investment needs of the business to service new contracts. Otherwise the company could find itself in the position of having to turn down tenders for new business in the future simply due to a lack of funding. By strengthening the balance sheet at this stage, Communisis was not constrained in seeking out business opportunities.

Assessing returns on capital

It only made sense to have a major equity fundraising if the company could generate returns on capital well above the costs of the equity issued. Otherwise Communisis would be destroying shareholder value. So to make sure the company was making a satisfactory return on new contracts, the board appraised all contracts on the basis that they generated:

- An internal objective of delivering double-digit operating margins on sales.

- An internal rate of return of 20 per cent on capital employed.

- Maximum payback period of three years.

In other words, the rates of return on the new contracts were well in excess of both the cost of the new equity being issued and the blended cost of the company's capital. Shareholders clearly liked the rationale for the fundraising, and following the announcement of the placing and open offer, shares in Communisis rose a further 20 per cent to 55p by early March 2013. The shares also enjoyed an earnings expansion, as the forward earnings multiple had risen to 11 as investors reappraised the investment risk. It also provided bumper capital returns as the share price had almost doubled on my original advice to buy a year earlier.

Key lessons to learn:

- **Assess return on capital.** There is little point in a company raising equity for expansion if it is destroying shareholder value by generating a net return below the cost of the new capital raised.

- **Assess working capital requirements.** A company growing profits through new contracts will require additional working capital to fund the new business. Check whether headroom on credit facilities is large enough for the company to fund this growth.

- **Raising new equity.** Check whether lenders are reducing credit lines as part of the equity raise. It is one thing for a company to issue new shares to provide the working capital to grow profits; it's quite another for lenders to slash credit lines.

4

Capitalising on capital returns

There are a host of ways companies can return capital to shareholders and it is possible to make money from nearly all of them. Share buy-backs, tender offers and special dividends are the three that I focus on most. For the purposes of this chapter, I will illustrate specific examples of how these capital returns can be exploited by investors.

---

case study 8

Tender offers

Shares in LMS Capital, an investment company with over 30 years' experience in private equity and development capital, have not proved a great investment over the years, which explains why they were trading 35 per cent below book value of 83p a share when I unearthed their potential a couple of years ago (*Investors Chronicle*, 'Capital returns', 14 February 2011). Undoubtedly, the shares would have continued to trade at a deep discount to net asset value if it had not been for the fact that the board decided to sell off all the company's investments and return capital to shareholders.

This process would take time since LMS's portfolio of investments was worth £236m, including quoted equities; unlisted investments; and funds mainly exposed to UK property, US buyouts and venture capital. Still, the company was not a forced seller since it had no borrowings and uncalled fund commitments were more than covered by the cash pile. In turn, this paved the way for capital to be returned to shareholders as the divestment process unfolded.

And this is where the company was really smart. That's because although its shares had risen by 17 per cent to 64p in the following 16 months after I first highlighted the potential for share price gains, they were still trading at a hefty 27 per cent discount to net asset value when I revisited the investment case (*Investors Chronicle*, 'Time to capitalise on LMS Capital', 25 June 2012). A few months later, and LMS announced a tender offer at 85p a share in order to return £40m of its £51.5m net cash pile to shareholders.

Win-win situation

This was a win-win situation because shareholders not only benefited from selling up to 17 per cent of their shareholdings at book value of 85p, but could then use all of the proceeds to buy back LMS shares in the market at around 67p, which would lower their entry price. Moreover, returning capital by a tender process created a floor for the share price as the portfolio was wound down and reduced the investment risk.

It also created an arbitrage opportunity for other investors and not just existing shareholders to exploit. That's because any investor could buy shares in LMS Capital before the closing date for the tender offer and make immediate capital gains simply by tendering the shares at a much higher price.

Key lessons to learn:

■ **Tender offer allows realisation of cash**. Investors can sell part of their holdings and then use the funds received from the company to buy back shares at the lower market price to reduce the average cost of their holding.

■ **Tender offer supports share price and narrows discount to book value**. That's because additional buying of shares in the open market from investors using funds received from their tendered shares drives up the price. In the case of LMS, by March 2013 its share price had risen a further 10 per cent to 74p, which narrowed the discount to book value to 13 per cent.

Dividends

Most companies still pay out cash dividends in the traditional way every six months to their shareholder base, but a growing number of treasury and finance departments are being smarter in the way they return cash to their shareholders.

For instance, FTSE 250 property companies Raven Russia and CLS Holdings both use a tender offer process to buy in shares well above the market price from their investor base and in lieu of a traditional dividend. To illustrate how you can make money from this, consider the example of Raven Russia, a company I made a strong investment case for in March 2013 (*Investors Chronicle*, 'A major buy signal beckons', 11 March 2013).

---

case study 9

Capitalising on dividends

Raven Russia is a decent-yielding share offering an historic dividend yield of around 5.7 per cent, based on a total payout of 3.75p a share and a share price of 66p. However, instead of paying this amount as a cash dividend, the company invited shareholders to tender their shares. In the 2012 financial year the company used a tender offer to make an interim distribution by inviting shareholders to tender one in every 49 shares held at 75p, equivalent to a dividend of 1.5p per share. Raven Russia also made a final distribution of 2.25p by way of a tender offer of one share in every 33 held at 75p. With the company's net asset value around 125 US cents, or 83p a share at current exchange rates, this method of returning capital has four main benefits.

■ **Enables profit taking without depressing share price**. Investors are able to bank gains on their holdings without adversely affecting the company's share price. In fact, Raven Russia shareholders had the opportunity to sell more than their pro rata entitlement (up to their entire holding of ordinary shares) to the extent that other shareholders tendered less than their pro rata entitlement.

■ **Boosts net asset value.** Because the shares were being purchased through the tender offer at a price below the 83p-a-share book value, but above the share price of 66p when Raven Russia announced the distribution, this had the effect of increasing the company's net asset value per share.

■ **Arbitrage opportunity.** Shareholders were able to tender their shares at 75p and then use the proceeds to buy them back in the market at 66p to reduce their average buy-in price. They could also increase the size of their holdings by using the profit made on this trade.

■ **Supports the share price.** Perhaps, most importantly, this tender process has the effect of raising the open market price of the company's shares as some investors will use the cash proceeds from the tender offer to buy back the shares they have tendered in the market, but at a lower price. This has the effect of forcing up the price, which narrows the share price discount to book value and provides gains for all shareholders.

And, like the example of LMS Capital, the tender offer process creates an arbitrage opportunity for all investors to exploit, by simply buying shares in a company before the closing date of the tender offer. In Raven Russia's case, the closing date to be eligible to tender shares was seven weeks after the company announced its full-year results in March 2013. So an outside investor could buy shares, and then immediately tender part of the holding back to the company at the higher tender price and sell the remainder in the market after the tender closes.

In some instances, it is possible to benefit from an increase in the company's share price when it comes to sell the untendered shares in the open market. That's because there is technical buying pressure from shareholders topping up their shareholdings by buying back the shares they have just tendered, but at a much lower price, in the open market. And, of course, there is the guaranteed capital gain on the shares tendered.

Share buy-back programmes

Not all share buy-back programmes add value and some actually destroy value if the earnings yield – the reciprocal of the PE ratio – is below the cost of capital being used to carry out the buy-back. Or, put it another way, if a company's shares are too highly rated relative to the cost of the debt being used to buy back shares, then apart from propping up the share price, the programme will actually destroy shareholder value because it dilutes earnings per share.

However, when it comes to investment companies the equation is far simpler. That's because if a company's shares are priced on a discount to book value then a buy-back programme actually increases the book value – the benchmark on which investment companies are valued. And where trading volumes are relatively low, the action of a company aggressively buying its own shares can force up its share price to the benefit of all shareholders. To illustrate how this works in practice, consider the example of Aim-traded company Crystal Amber, which I first recommended buying shares in at 91p two years ago (*Investors Chronicle*, ' Amber Alert', 10 May 2011).

---

case study 10

How to capitalise on share buy-back programmes

Between mid December 2012 and the end of March 2013 Crystal Amber purchased 2.66m shares, or 4.4 per cent of its share capital, in 11 transactions at prices between 100p and 114p. The average buy-in price was 107.4p, which compares favourably with a net asset value of 120p a share at the end of December 2012, and 128p a share at the end of March 2013. Moreover, Crystal Amber's share price has risen by 18 per cent from 100p to 118p since the start of the buy-back programme, so narrowing the share price discount markedly to net asset value, to the benefit of all shareholders.

The lesson here is that a modest amount of share buying by a company can have an accentuated impact on its share price if daily trading volumes are normally low. Therefore, by monitoring how share buy-back programmes affect the share prices of small-cap companies you can ride on the coat-tails of the company's buy-back programme by buying shares in these specific special situations.

5

Sum-of-the-parts valuations

I t is fair to say that my investment style is that of a classic value investor. Primarily I look for companies that I believe are being undervalued by investors even though the quality of their assets is sound. In particular, I look for businesses trading well below their net asset value or where the sum-of-the-parts valuations reveal hidden value in a company's assets. This may take time to realise, but over the years some of the best gains made on shares I have recommended in *Investors Chronicle* have been on investment companies trading at deep discounts to book value even though there is a plan in place to realise that value.

This is an important point because many listed companies are valued way below book value and in lots of cases this can be justified by a number of factors. These include:

- Low growth in sales and profits.

- Low returns on capital employed.

- High debt levels.

- Relatively high cost of capital employed.

- Poor cash generation.

- EPS and dividend growth rates below peers and market average.

However, when a company is aiming to sell off its investments in order to return cash to shareholders this changes the ball game completely. The focus is then on the time it is going to take to realise the investments and the likely proceeds thereof.

It also brings into focus the underlying value in the company's assets. With cash being returned to shareholders it reduces investment risk, by limiting the share price downside. But most important of all, the prospect of a large capital return is just the catalyst investors need to spark a rerating to close the share price discount to net asset value.

case study 11

Share price discounts and catalysts for reratings

Shares in B.P. Marsh & Partners, a niche venture capital provider to early-stage financial services businesses, were trading at a huge discount to book value, and had been for as long as I could remember when I highlighted the investment opportunity in the autumn of 2012 (*Investors Chronicle*, 'Hyper value buy', 26 October 2012).

What made B.P. Marsh such an interesting, and remarkably low-risk investment at that point in time was that it owned a 13.8 per cent stake in global insurance broker Hyperion Insurance Group, one of the fastest growing companies in the UK. Established in 1994, Hyperion specialises in wholesale and retail broking, reinsurance broking and underwriting in more than 50 countries around the world.

Hyperion had not only been building up scale by acquisition, but was growing strongly on an underlying basis too. In fact, in the financial year ending 30 September 2012, Hyperion increased like-for-like revenues on continuing operations by 12 per cent to £111m, an increase of 42 per cent including acquisitions, and raised cash profits by 40 per cent to £20.6m. This more than justified the £225m valuation placed on the business and the £31.1m carrying value for B.P. Marsh's stake.

Moreover, the value was set to be crystallised when Hyperion floated on the London Stock Exchange, which was expected within 12 months. What made this such a compelling investment is that B.P. Marsh's stake in Hyperion was worth £4.7m more than its own market value of £26.4m, even though the company was not in financial distress. Indeed, B.P. Marsh had net cash on the balance sheet of £3.3m. This meant that, despite holding the valuable stake in Hyperion, the company was being valued on an eye-watering 50 per cent discount to its July 2012 net asset value of £52m.

In other words, the £48m investment portfolio, of which the stake in Hyperion accounted for a two-thirds weighting, offered rock-solid asset backing for anyone buying B.P. Marsh & Partners' shares. To put that into perspective, it meant that £25.6m of investments (of which £3.3m was in cash), were in the price for nothing, including all of B.P. Marsh's other holdings, worth £16.9m, in eight other insurance companies. The low valuation placed on the equity of B.P. Marsh also failed to acknowledge the company's enviable track record of increasing net assets at an underlying annual compound growth rate of 12 per cent after running costs, realisations, losses and distributions since the company was established in 1990.

It didn't take long for the anomalous valuation to correct itself. In fact, by the end of March 2013, when B.P. Marsh announced that it had sold off 80 per cent of its stake in Hyperion for £29.2m, ahead of a likely flotation of the insurer, shares in B.P. Marsh had soared by 45 per cent to 130p in under six months. This markedly closed the share price discount to book value of around 185p.

Key lessons to learn:

■ **Catalyst in place for a rerating**. It was reasonable to assume that the share price discount to net asset value would narrow as the flotation of Hyperion approached.

■ **Significant upside potential**. B.P. Marsh was trading on a huge discount to net asset value so, even if the discount only narrowed by half, the share price upside would be almost 50 per cent.

■ **No financial distress**. B.P. Marsh was in a net cash position so was not a forced seller of any of its investments.

■ **Excellent management track record**. B.P. Marsh had grown the company's net assets 13-fold over a period of 23 years, which is testament to the quality of management and its investment portfolio.

■ **Hyperion was growing strongly**. As a result, this is the type of business institutional investors would want to hold following the international public offering (IPO), so there was potential upside on the carrying value of B.P. Marsh's stake in Hyperion once it listed on the main London market. It also meant that there would be trade buyers for B.P. Marsh's stake ahead of the IPO.

case Study 12

Calculating likely capital returns

The other way a company can sharply close the share price discount to the book value of its assets is by winding itself up and returning the cash proceeds to shareholders. Corporate activity of this nature is likely to be noticed by other investors and make them reassess the investment case.

In the case of Spark Ventures, an Aim-traded investment company focused on technology and new media, the board had a stated deadline of March 2014 to sell off its investment portfolio when I highlighted the buying opportunity in the summer of 2012 (*Investors Chronicle*, 'Spark for a rerating', 10 July 2012). It was making good progress at the time, having already returned £16.4m, or 4.1p a share, of cash to shareholders in the previous three years.

Moreover, adjusting for those capital distributions and the company's net asset value had risen by 66 per cent between October 2009 and March 2012, so the portfolio was performing well. But despite sitting on a cash-rich balance sheet, and one that was set to receive a significant boost in the weeks ahead, Spark Ventures' shares, at 9.5p, were trading around 40 per cent below book value of 16p a share.

| Table 5.1 | Spark Ventures' investment portfolio July 2012 |

Portfolio company name	Pro forma value (£m)	Pro forma value per share (p)
IMIMobile	15.9	3.9
Kobalt Music	8.8	2.1
Mind Candy	3.2	0.8
notonthehighstreet.com	10.2	2.5
OpenX	2.5	0.6
Firebox	1.0	0.2
DEM Solutions	1.7	0.4
Gambling Compliance	1.8	0.4
Aspex	0.0	0.0
Academia	0.9	0.2
MBlox	0.5	0.1
Other Holdings < £500,000	1.0	0.2
Total	47.4	11.6
Pro forma cash or cash equivalents		
Balance sheet cash 31 Mar 2012	7.0	1.7
Aspex Loan repayment	1.0	0.2
notonthehighstreet.com share sale	0.8	0.2
Kobalt share sale	3.5	0.9
Aspex share sale	7.0	1.7
Pro forma total cash	**19.3**	**4.7**
Liabilities	1.1	0.3
Pro forma net assets	65.6	16

Source: *Investors Chronicle*, 'Spark for a rerating', 10 July 2012

So with the company only capitalised at £39m, this meant more than £26m of assets were in the price for free. Now that huge discount to book value would be justified if the 15 investments Spark held (worth £58.7m) were of dubious quality. But this was clearly not the case.

For instance, Spark's stake in London-based internet marketplace www.notonthehighstreet.com had surged from £4.5m to £10.2m between September 2011 and March 2012 using the valuation Fidelity Investments bought in at as part of a funding round. Spark was also a founder investor in Mind Candy, the company behind Moshi Monsters, a leading developer of skill-enhancing games designed to enable children to connect safely with each other in a social network. The company had sold half its holding in Mind Candy, but still retained a £3.2m investment.

I calculated that following a number of disposals, Spark's cash pile would swell from £7m of net cash on its balance sheet at its March 2012 financial year-end to around £19.3m that summer. To put this into some perspective, around 4.7p a share of the company's 16p book value was in effect cash, which mitigated the risk in buying Spark's shares at 9.5p. Moreover, the 4.8p-a-share difference was more than covered by holdings in notonthehighstreet.com, Mind Candy and Kobalt (the world's leading music publisher), which had a combined worth of £22.2m, or 5.4p a share, and were easily realisable.

Importantly, the interests of management and shareholders were well aligned as non-executive director Michael Whitaker, previously founding chief executive of Spark, was one of the largest shareholders, holding a 5.6 per cent stake. There was also a large financial incentive for the management team carrying out the disposals to get the best possible prices because they were entitled to 15 per cent of future distributions made to Spark shareholders, once 11p a share had been paid out, falling to 5 per cent, once 14p a share had been returned. That was a potential £3m payout which had been agreed by all of Spark's major shareholders.

| Table 5.2 | Spark Ventures' major shareholders in July 2012 |

Shareholder	Shareholding	Percentage
M&G Investment Management	86,366,122	21.02%
RWC Partners	45,874,424	11.16%
Michael Whitaker	22,832,153	5.56%
River & Mercantile Asset Management	18,688,466	4.55%
Ennismore Fund Management	18,468,950	4.50%
Thomas Teichman	16,434,138	4.00%
Lobbenberg Family	16,350,000	3.98%
Henderson Global Investors	16,312,500	3.97%
Ingot Capital Management	15,250,000	3.71%
Total	**256,576,753**	**62.45%**

Source: *Investors Chronicle*, 'Spark for a rerating', 10 July 2012

It was my view that, as soon as other investors realised the scale of a likely capital return, Spark's shares would enjoy a significant rerating to narrow the share price discount to net asset value. And this is exactly what happened, as Spark announced a few months later, in the autumn of 2012, that it would return £10.3m, or 2.5p a share, in early 2013. This news proved the catalyst for a near 40 per cent rerating in Spark's share price.

Key lessons to learn:

■ Share price backed by substantial cash holdings.

■ Major investments could be sold easily and turned into cash.

■ Management and shareholder interests aligned in disposal process given management incentives to achieve best sale prices.

■ Major shareholders had agreed disposals and there was a specific timescale to complete the process.

■ Level of cash return set to be announced within months so catalyst in place for share price rerating within a modest time scale.

case study 13

Timing the entry point

As the share price reratings of B.P. Marsh and Spark Ventures clearly show, timing the entry point is critical if you are to maximise returns over the shortest possible time frame.

A classic example of timing the entry point to perfection is Aim-traded, Russia-focused private equity company Aurora Russia, of which I noted the investment potential in early 2013 (*Investors Chronicle*, 'Time to play Russian roulette', 4 February 2013).

Aurora had proved a dire investment since listing in April 2006 when the company raised £75m at 100p a share. Even investors who subscribed to a placing at 40p a share in 2010 were still under water with the shares trading at 30p in early 2013, less than half book value. However, I noted that the company's board had made a commitment to shareholders in August 2011 to realise "tangible value" within two years, so they had at most six months left to realise value from the four remaining investments held.

Bearing this in mind, what caught my eye was an announcement that the company had appointed an investment bank to act as broker and nominated adviser (Nomad) for Aurora's 92.8 per cent owned subsidiary, OSG, which planned to list on the Alternative Investment Market (Aim) after the company published full-year results for the financial year to 31 March 2013. In other words, there was a plan in place to crystallise the value in the assets of the company in the near future.

I also thought the float would appeal to UK investors since OSG is a fast-growing records management provider with operations in Russia, Poland, Ukraine and Kazakhstan. It is a profitable operation, having reported cash profits of £1.7m on revenues of £11m in the six months to September 2012. So with OSG's annualised cash profits around £3.4m and growing fast, a carrying value of £29.9m on the 92.8 per cent stake held by Aurora looked sensible.

The investment case was even more compelling, given that Aurora's £29.9m stake in OSG, worth 27p a share, accounted for 43 per cent of the company's net asset value of £70m, or 62.3p a share. To put that into perspective, Aurora's shares were trading at only 30.5p in February 2013, valuing the company at £34.3m, or less than half book value.

Factor in net cash of £2.1m on Aurora's balance sheet and £700,000 of property assets up for sale, and the share price was covered entirely by property, cash and the stake in OSG, which left holdings in three remaining investments in the price for free. These included a 26 per cent stake in Unistream Bank and a 24.3 per cent stake in Superstoy, a leading DIY retailer in Russia, which combined were on the books for around £28m. Importantly, there was a plan in place to crystallise this value, as Aurora's board was in discussions to dispose of the assets and expected to have concrete news to report before the company's year-end results were announced.

So by my reckoning, Aurora had potential to provide 50 per cent share price upside within a six-month period with limited downside risk. I calculated this figure by:

- Conservatively applying a 40 per cent haircut to the carrying value of Unistream Bank and Superstoy in a fire sale scenario to value these stakes at 14.8p a share.

- Assuming an exit from its subsidiary, Flexinvest Bank, would bring in £9m (or 8p a share) after deducting the £3m value of the bank licence (these figures had been estimated by broker Jefferies).

- Valuing the stake in OSG at £25m, or 22p a share, to reflect likely selling in the after-market when it demerged.

- Assuming Aurora's cash on the balance sheet, property assets and trade receivables would cover all liabilities, including management fees, realisation fees and operating expenses. It is important to factor in wind-up costs and ongoing operational expenses when estimating a likely break-up value of any company.

Other investors had also been eyeing up OSG, because only three weeks after I had highlighted the investment case for Aurora, the company announced that Elbrus Capital, a private equity business in Russia and the CIS, had agreed to acquire OSG. The deal was worth up to $47.8m, or £30.3m, before transaction costs (*Investors Chronicle*, 'From Russia with profit', 25 February 2013). This not only avoided the need to float OSG on Aim, but meant that all of Aurora's shareholders would be able to exit the investment in OSG at its full carrying value in the company's accounts – something that would not have been possible if OSG had listed on Aim. That's because the likely selling pressure would have driven OSG's share price down below its float price and net asset value.

With the investment in OSG bringing in 27p a share (albeit 3p a share of that is dependent on the March 2014 earn-out terms being met and a further 2.4p a share will be held in escrow subject to any warranty claim), shares in Aurora rocketed from 30.5p to 39p by the end of February, providing a near-30 per cent return in only three weeks.

Key lessons to learn:

■ The company's board had a deadline to make disposals, so there was a stated six-month timescale for any investment in Aurora shares.

■ Shares trading at half book value, which didn't accurately reflect the potential cash returns to shareholders.

■ Aurora was planning to list OSG separately on Aim within months, which would bring into focus the value in Aurora's other investments post the listing.

■ Even after conservatively valuing all the remaining investments using a 40 per cent discount to the book value of the assets in Aurora's latest reported accounts, the sum-of-the-parts valuation was still 50 per cent more than the company's share price.

6

Takeover targets and merger arbitrage

My balance-sheet-based approach to stock picking has the benefit of uncovering investment opportunities that are likely bid targets. This is especially the case with companies being valued on hefty discounts to net asset value even though there are few signs of financial distress.

When a company is being rated well below the current value of its assets, and in some cases on a deep discount to replacement value, then it's highly likely that activist shareholders and potential bidders will be running the rule over them. One catalyst for a bidder to emerge and take advantage of the attractive valuation on offer is an improvement in trading in the target company. This mitigates the investment risk for the acquirer.

One method of seeking out likely bid targets is to focus on good-quality companies with strong balance sheets offering potential for an earnings recovery, but where the assets are modestly priced relative to book value. Even if this is the case, a takeover is unlikely to happen unless the majority shareholders can be persuaded to part with their paper, and there is a willing buyer.

So to increase your chances of uncovering a potential takeover target, it is best to focus on companies with specific characteristics.

Key characteristics of potential bid targets

■ **Directors' shareholdings are relatively low**. There is an incentive for directors to recommend a takeover as they benefit from upside on their share option packages, which represent a far greater proportion of their financial interest in the company.

■ **No single shareholder controls a majority stake in the target company**. This can act as a major stumbling block in a takeover situation. In order to improve the odds of a predator being able to persuade shareholders to accept its offer, then it's best to focus on companies where the major shareholders control relatively small stakes.

■ **Majority of shareholders believe the company is significantly undervalued**. As a result, they will be more inclined to entertain bid approaches in order to boost the value of their holdings.

■ **Financial performance has been below that of peers**. This raises questions as to whether the company would be better managed by another management team.

■ **Bid target would benefit from being part of a larger entity**. There can be clear cost advantages of merging with a much larger group, including cost savings, cross-selling opportunities and economies of scale in manufacturing and head office functions.

■ **More cost-effective for acquirer to bid for target company**. This is especially the case when the assets on the balance sheet of the bid target are being valued at below replacement cost or where it would take a considerable amount of time for the acquirer to build the same business from scratch.

■ **Sector characterised by a number of larger companies**. This offers scope for consolidation as smaller businesses are taken over.

The financial rewards of finding a potential bid target can be impressive too, as the case of Aim-traded sweets manufacturer Zetar clearly illustrates (*Investors Chronicle*, 'Supreme value stocks', 30 April 2012).

case study 14

Recovery and bid potential not priced in

Disappointing trading over the all-important Easter period forced Aim-traded confectionary and snack food producer Zetar to issue its second profit warning of the year in the spring of 2012. As a result, adjusted pre-tax profits for the 12 months to end-April 2012 were expected to come in at £5.5m, significantly less than the £7.1m analysts had been forecasting at the start of 2012 – and well below the £6.6m they had forecast following the first profit warning in January.

It also meant that Zetar's full-year profits would be down on the £6.7m reported in the year to April 2011. The news sent the shares down sharply, and at 185p, they were priced 50 per cent below net asset value and on less than six times earnings per share of 32p for the financial year.

Although investor sentiment had taken a knock, the valuation was very attractive once you factored in the potential for an earnings recovery in the new financial year to April 2013, and one that looked highly likely to take place. That's because Zetar had been winning contracts with a number of customers for both branded and private-label products; the company's confectionary business was set to get a boost from sales of London 2012 Olympic biscuits, the contract on which had been deferred and accounted for part of the above-profit shortfall; and a cost reduction plan was expected to reduce overheads by £600,000. Moreover, and reassuringly, a tight control of the company's finances meant borrowings had been reduced by almost a third to £10m in the year to April 2012, so balance sheet gearing was only 21 per cent of shareholders' funds of £47m.

Factoring in the contract wins, the interest savings on reduced borrowings and the cost savings mentioned above, several analysts predicted that pre-tax profits would recover to £7.2m in the 12 months to April 2013 to produce EPS of over 40p. On that basis, the shares were being priced on a miserly 4.5 times earnings estimates for the coming financial year. Furthermore, with the benefit of weak comparatives following a period of disappointing trading, Zetar looked well-placed to produce the good news story needed to provide the catalyst for a significant share price rerating.

Other investors had realised this too, because five months later, in early October 2012, the company received a bid from Hamburg-based speciality food group Zertus. The cash offer of 297p a share valued Zetar at £42.7m, a 9 per cent discount to its last reported net asset value and equated to a take-out price of 7.5 times analysts' EPS estimates for the financial year to April 2013. Add in a 3p-a-share final dividend and the consideration of 300p a share represented a 62 per cent return in only five months.

Key lessons to learn:

- Zetar's assets were being priced below replacement value prior to the bid.

- Business was in recovery following a poor financial performance in the previous year.

- Zetar could easily service its debt from operating cash flow, which would appeal to an acquirer wanting to gear up the company's balance sheet to fund the acquisition.

- Comparatives were weak, so even if a bidder didn't emerge, there was a fair chance that the shares would re-rate as investors reassessed the investment case in light of an improving trading performance.

- Zetar's six largest shareholders owned just 33 per cent of the shares.

- Combined shareholdings of Zetar's management team and board represented only 13.6 per cent of the issued share capital.

- Buyout vehicle offered managers equity in the new company, so they were incentivised to consider the takeover approach seriously.

- The food producers sector is dominated by large groups, which can easily afford to buy smaller businesses to add new product lines and exploit cross-selling opportunities with existing customer base.

Playing the takeover game

It also pays to keep a close eye on companies that have already received a bid approach to try to capitalise on potential investment opportunities. But there are several factors you need to consider first before playing the takeover game.

■ **Weigh up the risk and rewards.** To do this, assess the probability of the indicative bid turning into a formal takeover and consider all the reasons why the bidder would want to close the deal. Then decide if there are compelling reasons for it not to, since this would put your capital at risk.

■ **Calculate the likely share price downside if the bidder walks away**. Then compare this figure with the upside potential if the deal completes. The ratio of upside potential to downside risk has to be in your favour, otherwise the capital returns are simply not large enough for the risk you are taking on.

■ **Estimate the likely time frame for a formal offer to be made by the acquirer**. This is important because the longer it takes for a takeover situation to resolve itself, the longer you will have your capital tied up, which in turn, impacts on the annualised return on the capital you will be investing ahead of a formal announcement of a bid.

To show how this can work in practice consider the case of Aim-traded Just Retirement, a financial services group specialising in the retirement sector, which received an indicative bid approach from Avalon Acquisitions, a fund formed by private equity group Permira. Admittedly, this was a long-running saga as Just Retirement first announced a bid approach in November 2008, but it looked as though the end was in sight by the summer of 2009 when I highlighted a potentially profitable trading opportunity (*Investors Chronicle*, 'An investment to retire on', 20 June 2009).

case study 15

Merger arbitrage

Avalon had clearly been doing the rounds of institutions and had the backing of shareholders controlling 52.3 per cent of Just Retirement's share capital for a cash offer of 76p a share, valuing the company at £225m. So having spent the time and effort gathering support for a takeover, it seemed highly likely that Avalon would close the deal by launching a formal bid. And with Just Retirement's shares being offered in the market at 67.5p there was a potential 12 per cent share price upside on offer by buying the shares ahead of a formal bid announcement being made.

The indicative cash offer looked sensibly priced too, representing a premium to Just Retirement's embedded value of 45p a share (this measure of net asset value takes into account the value of the annuity policies issued). It was easy to see why Avalon was attracted by Just Retirement since the company's sales of annuity policies and equity release mortgage advances had hit record levels, buoyed by annuity sales. The equity release mortgage business was also a decent money-spinner for Just Retirement; the company had advanced around 9,000 lifetime mortgages in the previous four years to give it a market share of 13 per cent of a niche lending market worth £1.2bn.

True, there was a risk that Avalon would not issue a formal offer, but this appeared slim given that 52 per cent shareholder Langholm Capital had already given its undertaking to back the takeover. In the event, Avalon made a formal offer at 76p a share to provide investors with a decent 12 per cent return in under four months. Repeat this process three times a year and that return equates to an eye-watering annualised return on invested capital of 40 per cent.

Key lessons to learn:

■ Just Retirement's shares offered as much upside potential as downside risk so the risk:reward ratio was adequate.

■ Acquirer already had backing of a major and controlling shareholder, which improved the odds of a formal bid being launched.

■ Acquirer had been doing due diligence for an extensive period of time and would have incurred substantial fees in the process, so was clearly committed to doing a deal.

■ Indicative cash offer was sensibly priced to entice other shareholders to accept the offer.

■ Business was performing strongly, which mitigates financial risk for the acquirer.

Arbitraging anomalies

Another way of playing the takeover game is to look for bid targets that have received indicative or formal bids, where there is an arbitrage opportunity to exploit by buying shares in the target to benefit from potential capital gains in the shares of the acquirer.

A great example of this occurred in early 2009 when property company Raven Mount received an all-share offer, and a rather complicated one at that, from Raven Russia, a developer of warehouses and logistic parks in Russia (*Investors Chronicle*, 'Merger arbitrage', 30 April 2009).

case study 16

Playing the merger arbitrage game

The offer tabled to Raven Mount shareholders consisted of 0.525 units in Raven Russia, comprising one preference share and one call warrant, for each Raven Mount share held. The preference shares have a par value of 100p and pay a quarterly coupon of 3p payable in arrears. The call warrants have an exercise price of 25p per Raven Russia ordinary share and expire in April 2019.

So with shares in Raven Russia trading at 17.5p in April 2009, the warrants only had time value and no intrinsic value, reflecting the fact that they had 10 years to run and the fixed exercise price of 25p was well above the market price of Raven Russia shares. That said, the warrants clearly had some value and market makers priced them at a mid-price of 6.5p, albeit on a horrible 3p to 10p bid-offer spread. The preference shares were trading at a mid-price of 100p on a much tighter spread of 98p to 102p.

This meant that an owner of one unit in Raven Russia (comprising one preference share and one warrant) would receive 101p by selling in the market. On the same basis, any investor buying shares in Raven Mount and immediately accepting the offer from Raven Russia of 0.525 units for every Raven Mount share held could then sell these units for 53p. The latter figure was highly relevant because Raven Mount shares were trading in the market on a bid-offer spread of 36p to 42p, so the market price had yet to adjust to reflect the value of the offer on the table.

In fact, the 11p-a-share difference between the offer price of Raven Mount shares and the market price of Raven Russia's preference and warrants provided an attractive 26 per cent potential capital gain to any investor buying Raven Mount shares. The investor could then accept the offer from Raven Russia and then immediately sell the Raven Russia preference and warrants in the market. The best part was that this profit could be realised in a relatively short period of time since Raven Mount's offer had over 64 per cent acceptances, so was on course to go unconditional in a matter of weeks.

> True, investors had to calculate how easy it would be to sell the warrants and preference shares, but liquidity was not an issue in the secondary market since Raven Russia had already raised £76.2m in a placing of new preference shares at 100p per unit.

Key lessons to learn:

- **High level of acceptances.** This meant the risk of the bid lapsing was negligible.

- **Significant upside potential.** The arbitrage opportunity meant there was a 26 per cent potential return to be made on capital invested.

- **Downside risk was low.** It was highly likely the bid would go unconditional and liquidity was good in Raven Russia's preference shares, which represented 98 per cent of the consideration received by Raven Mount shareholders. Therefore it was easy for investors to sell Raven Russia preference shares in the secondary market to book profits on the arbitrage trade.

- **High annualised return on capital invested.** Since the arbitrage trade could be executed in a matter of weeks from start to finish, the annualised return was very attractive.

7

Tell-tale signs of recovery plays

U
ltimately, it doesn't matter how lowly valued a company is, you need a spark for the share price to re-rate. The most likely one is the most obvious: an improvement in trading performance.

So to gauge how well a company is trading, I meticulously go through the last 18 months' interim reports, preliminary results statements and trading statements to work out the underlying trends and pinpoint key growth drivers in the business. This includes anticipating what company-specific newsflow is set to be released over the coming months, and estimating the likely implications for the share price based on a series of possible outcomes.

This is a very useful exercise, not to mention one that can also be financially rewarding, especially for companies that have gone through restructuring and have slimmed down their cost base. That's because modest increases in sales can have a disproportionately large impact on profitability as the operational gearing of the business kicks in. As a result, it can pay big dividends to buy into these special situations before other investors cotton on. But only if you know what to look for.

A great example of a recovery play, that exhibits all the characteristics I am looking for when I try to spot these golden nugget investment opportunities, is home shopping retailer Ideal Shopping Direct.

The tell-tale signs of a company in recovery mode

In the autumn of 2009 I noted that both the finance director and chief executive of one of the UK's leading home shopping retailers, Ideal Shopping Direct, had been digging deep into their pockets to purchase shares in their company (*Investors Chronicle*, 'Investing in an Ideal World', 12 October 2009).

In fact boss Mike Hancox had splashed out £400,000 purchasing 500,000 shares at 80p each, while finance director Ian Jebson had invested £32,000 buying 40,000 shares at the same price. Given that Ideal Shopping was only capitalised at £25.5m, this was a significant investment by these two insiders, and one that warranted further investigation.

Directors' backgrounds

The first thing I looked into was the background of the directors to find out their track records. In the case of Mr Hancox, he had been in the hot seat for 12 months, having been brought in to turn around a business that managed to post a loss of over £13m on £94.5m of sales in 2008. He had form in this area, having successfully turned around Otto UK, the world's largest home shopping retailer, prior to joining Ideal Shopping.

Analyse the accounts

I then ripped through the past 18 months of the company's accounts to analyse how the losses had come about. In the process, I calculated that £9.2m of that thumping loss of £13m resulted from what appeared to be an extensive kitchen sink operation. This is when the board reviews all the operations across the business and writes down the carrying value of assets, or takes one-off restructuring costs as exceptional items to clean the decks. As a result, the company is starting from a clean slate, which is worth noting because in recovery situations this can signal that there will be no more exceptional costs in the future. One-off charges not only dent reported profits, but also have implications for cash flow. So if you can mitigate the risk that all the exceptional costs have already been booked, this improves the chances that any improvement in the trading performance will not be held back by further one-off costs.

In the case of Ideal Shopping, the list of exceptional charges booked included: £2.75m of stock writedowns; £750,000 of restructuring costs; almost £700,000 for planning permission costs on an aborted new warehouse project; a £1.1m write-off on IT systems; a £1.5m goodwill impairment charge; and £750,000 for doubtful debts. There was even a £614,000 charge for loss of bank deposits following the collapse of Icelandic banks Kaupthing and Singer & Friedlander.

Cash generation is key

Clearly to make such a substantial personal investment in the shares of his company Mr Hancox must have believed that the restructuring programme was bearing fruit. Therefore, to ascertain whether this was in fact the case, it was necessary to determine whether the restructuring was improving the cash generation of the business. This is generally one of the first indicators of an improvement in the underlying trading performance.

I was not disappointed on this score, because by reducing warehousing facilities, and passing more of the inventory risk on to suppliers, Ideal Shopping had drastically reduced stock levels and working capital tied up in inventory. These measures contributed to a net cash inflow of £794,000 in the first six months of 2009. So although the company reported a first-half pre-tax loss of £1.2m, it actually generated £100,000 cash from operations, which bolstered its net cash pile to around £7.5m, or the equivalent of 30 per cent of the market capitalisation. This meant there were no financing issues to cloud the operational performance, and the business was no longer draining the company's cash.

Analyse the business model

Having stabilised the business, there was a plan in place to drive sales and return the company to profitability. To achieve this the management team was repositioning the business as a multi-channel retailer, in order to maximise earnings from a number of different revenue streams. These included Ideal Shopping's main channel, Ideal World, which is broadcast to 23m households on the Freeview, Sky, Virgin Media and Freesat platforms.

Interestingly, although a quarter of sales were online, predominantly from customers aged over 50, the main problem was not acquiring new customers, but improving both the product range and the customer experience. Moving the unpopular overseas call centre back to the UK and reintroducing customer agents for call handling, rather than using an automated phone ordering system, helped no end.

I therefore concluded that the main ingredients were in place for a strong turnaround. These were:

- Lower amounts of cash tied up in working capital.

- Improving cash flow generation.

- Improving product range to boost sales and significantly increase profits given the company's operational gearing.

Operational gearing

Ideal Shopping also ticked the right boxes when I estimated the upside potential of the turnaround. That's because the company had a relatively high fixed cost base so was highly operationally geared. This meant that with costs under tight control, small changes in sales would have an accentuated impact on profits as soon as the business moved back into the black. And this is exactly what happened as Ideal Shopping announced at the end of 2009 that it had turned profitable and, by January 2010, analysts were predicting it would make pre-tax profits of £2.5m in the financial year.

It was not just the bottom line that was improving either. As stock was turned into cash, the company's cash balances had almost doubled to £13.4m by January 2010, a significant sum of money considering Ideal Shopping was only being valued at £25m a few months previously.

Asset backing

It was worth noting that the company had other substantial assets, including freehold property worth £6.7m. An inspection of the notes to the company's accounts revealed that Ideal Shopping also had unutilised tax losses. Clearly these tax losses had value as it meant that Ideal Shopping wasn't going to have to pay corporation tax on profits earned for some time yet.

Share price momentum

Not surprisingly as other investors realised Ideal Shopping was in the early stages of a recovery, the company's share price soared. In fact, the price rose more than 60 per cent from around 86.5p when I highlighted the investment case in October 2009 to my initial target price of 140p by January 2010.

In the circumstances, and even though the shares had rocketed in a short time frame, I had no hesitation in raising my fair value target price to 200p a share. If achieved, this would have represented a rating of 15 times earnings estimates, net of the cash pile worth 46p a share. This rating may have seemed rich for a retailer, but it was in fact a reasonable valuation given the risk to earnings was weighted to the upside at this early stage of the company's recovery.

The end game

Over the next 12 months Ideal Shopping announced a series of trading statements that revealed the company was trading well ahead of analyst expectations. This reflected the geared effect on profits from modest rises in sales, given its high fixed cost base, and the fact that there was real sales momentum building up across the business as recovery took hold.

It was therefore not surprising that other companies were eyeing up Ideal Shopping's turnaround. In May 2011, the company succumbed to a private-equity-led cash offer of 220p a share, valuing the business at £78.3m. This provided a 150 per cent return to investors who had followed my advice to buy the shares 18 months previously.

Key lessons to learn:

The case of Ideal Shopping highlights several characteristics that help identify recovery plays. These include:

■ Management team with experience of successfully turning around previous businesses.

■ Director share buying as early signs of recovery in the business emerge.

■ Management review of business leads to a restructuring plan to lower cost base, realign operations and reduce working capital requirements.

■ Kitchen-sinking of accounts and large write-offs prior to turnaround becoming apparent.

■ Cash profitability ahead of a move into reported profits.

■ Improving stock control leads to sharp increases in cash flow and net cash position.

■ Operational gearing kicks in whereby rising sales on a lower cost base creates scope for an earnings upgrade cycle if sales exceed expectations.

■ Utilisation of tax losses mean earnings per share rise even faster than normal as profits recover due to absence of tax charge.

■ Substantial asset backing in place to give management time to turn around the business.

■ Low debt levels or net cash position mean limited financial risk associated with the investment.

Recovery plays and debt levels

Ideal Shopping had the benefit of being in a strong cash position before the recovery started, but most companies have borrowings. So if a company with significant debt levels appears to have a strong investment case, I always assess the cash generation of the business to decide whether underlying cash flows are sustainable to comfortably service borrowings. As a rule, I try to avoid companies where net debt is above 80 per cent of shareholders' funds and very rarely recommend buying shares when gearing is above 100 per cent in any recovery situation.

I also focus on companies trading at discounts to book value, for the simple reason that any improvement in the operational performance can act as a strong tailwind for a rerating to narrow the share price discount. That's because value investors will be more inclined to focus on the asset backing without having to worry about gearing levels and the company's ability to service its debt.

A classic example of this was Walker Greenbank, the luxury interior furnishings outfit whose brands include Morrison & Co, Harlequin and Zoffany, which was being valued on a near 40 per cent discount to net asset value when I first spotted the recovery potential in early 2010 (*Investors Chronicle*, 'Luxury at a bargain price', 8 February 2010).

---

case study 18

Best gains from lowly geared or cash-rich companies

At the time, Walker Greenbank's shareholders' funds of £21.4m comfortably exceeded its market value of £13.1m. This looked anomalous given that £8.6m of those assets were invested in property, including freehold buildings, land, plant and equipment.

These were not the only rock-solid assets on the balance sheet. Walker Greenbank also owns the valuable Arthur Anderson and William Morris archives of unique designs that generate a significant royalty income. Both were in the accounts at historic cost, so were in effect being undervalued. To put this anomalous valuation into some perspective, with the company's market value almost 40 per cent below its net asset value, those valuable archives, which were in the books at £5.8m, and around £2.5m of the freehold property assets were in the price for nothing.

Cash generation and falling debt levels

The investment case was even more compelling given that Walker Greenbank had strong cash generation. Tight stock control, lower capital expenditure and an improved trading performance meant that borrowing levels were falling sharply and were the equivalent of only 15 per cent of net assets. Lower debt not only reduces interest costs, but offers scope for increased investment in the business, which helps underpin sales and profits. And the signs were very promising as the company had used its robust cash flows to almost cut net debt in half, from £6.2m to £3.2m in the financial year to end January 2010.

However, it's one thing to have a rock-solid and lowly geared balance sheet, but Walker Greenbank needed to start growing revenues and profits again for the share price discount to book value to narrow. That's an important point to note, because like most manufacturing businesses Walker Greenbank is more operationally geared than many other companies given its high fixed cost base. As a result, modest increases in sales can have a profound impact on profits.

Understanding analyst forecasts and profit drivers

In early 2010, house broker Arden Partners expected the company's revenues to increase by 3.3 per cent from £60.4m to £62.4m in the financial year to 31 January 2011, but the impact on profits was far greater as the broker predicted pre-tax profits would surge from £2.3m to £3m. So a modest £2m uplift in sales had the effect of raising profits by £700,000. That's because an incremental amount of revenue was falling straight to the bottom line once the fixed costs had been covered. On this basis, the company's EPS was forecast to rise by over 26 per cent from 3p to 3.8p, which meant the shares were being rated on a very modest prospective PE ratio of 6.

It was also clear that if Walker Greenbank's management team could exceed the modest sales expectations of brokers, then there was upside potential in these earnings forecasts. That seemed a reasonable assumption to make considering the business was set to get a boost from its 150th anniversary and recently launched collections. Combined, the company's three main brands accounted for around two-thirds of total revenues and, aided by ongoing investment in new products, Walker Greenbank had been outperforming its peers.

The performance of the company's manufacturing business, accounting for the balance of revenues, was key to the turnaround. Having cut the cost base in 2009 when third-party sales were badly impacted during the recession, the business had been benefiting from restocking as their clients rebuilt inventory levels. There was also a shift in consumer tastes towards colour, which boosted demand for printed fabrics. Walker Greenbank's wallcoverings business was able to respond quickly to meet the changing needs of customers.

With a higher level of operational gearing due to a lower cost base, a greater proportion of manufacturing sales were dropping down to the bottom line. So much so, that the company's pre-tax profits rose four-fold to £2.1m in the six months to end July 2010, on sales up 13 per cent to £33m. This accounted for two-thirds of the full-year profit forecasts at the time and forced a raft of analyst earnings upgrades.

Earnings upgrade cycle

Post the half-year results, brokerage Oriel Securities raised its estimates by around 14 per cent and predicted that Walker Greenbank's pre-tax profits would rise from £2.3m to £3.7m in the 12 months to end January 2011. These estimates were based on annual sales increasing by around £5m to £65.1m. On this basis, full-year EPS was expected to rise from 3p to 4.7p.

In the event, the company smashed those upgraded estimates and lifted revenues by 14 per cent to £68.8m in the financial year to January 2011. And reflecting the operational gearing and boost to margins of the incremental increases in sales, operating profits soared by 77 per cent to £4.5m in the 12-month period. Cash flow generated from operations of £4.5m was equally robust, which enabled debt to be reduced even further. It also paved the way for a sharp rise in the dividend and significant share buy-backs, which in turn boosted earnings per share. That's because with the shares trading on such a low earnings multiple – 10 times earnings estimates in early 2011 – using cash flow to repurchase shares in the market and shrink the issued share capital had the effect of raising EPS for the remaining shares in issue.

The earnings upgrade cycle was not lost on investors: shares in Walker Greenbank soared by 120 per cent in the 18 months after my first buy recommendation in February 2010, and in the process, rerated from a sizeable share price discount to book value to a substantial premium. The PE ratio rose from less than six to around 10 within a year, so investors riding the earnings recovery story also benefited from the market attributing a higher rating to the profits that Walker Greenbank earned.

Key lessons to learn:

- **Limit financial risk.** Lowly geared companies underpinned by strong balance sheets and substantial asset backing reduce the financial risk associated with any investment.

- **Improving operational performance**. It is far easier to create a virtuous circle whereby operating cash flow is recycled back into the business, used to pay down debt, or returned to shareholders through share buy-backs and dividends, for lowly geared or cash-rich companies than for highly indebted companies.

- **Operational gearing.** This works both ways as falls in profits in periods of poor trading can be easily reversed when sales pick up again. Always estimate the impact on operating profits of changes in sales to determine the level of operational gearing a company offers.

- **Operational cash flow.** Avoid companies with poor cash flow performance – especially those where increases in operating profits are not being converted into improving operating cash flow.

- **Expansion of earnings multiple**. By reducing financial risk, improvements in operational performance can feed through to an expansion of the earnings multiple investors are willing to pay for a company's shares. In the case of Walker Greenbank, the rerating would not have been as great if debt levels had been significantly higher at the start of the recovery, as this would have introduced far more risk to the investment and deterred investors from valuing the shares on a higher earnings multiple.

- **Identify potential drivers for earnings upgrade cycle**. Potential drivers include growth opportunities to exploit new markets; restocking cycles; new products; structural changes in an industry; growth in emerging markets overseas; changes in fiscal and monetary policy.

8

Riding 'earnings upgrade cycles'

I n the previous chapter I outlined some of the key characteristics of companies in recovery mode and what to look for to identify them. Even if you don't manage to get in on the ground floor, it's always possible to play the upside by riding on the coat-tails of a company's improving operational performance.

The Holy Grail for investors is to identify companies with the potential to turn an early-stage recovery story into a multi-month earnings upgrade cycle. This is when a company issues a series of upbeat trading announcements that force analysts to repeatedly upgrade their earnings estimates. Fortunately, it is far easier to identify companies that are in earnings upgrade cycles than you would think. There are 10 key characteristics I look for.

■ **Potential to boost sales by exploiting new markets.**

■ **Cross-selling opportunities.** These may result directly from acquisitions or simply by better management of existing operations which had previously been run as independent business units.

■ **Restocking cycles.** This is when a company's end customers have run inventories down to low levels, as was the case in the aftermath of the global stock market crash, and deepening financial crisis in the autumn of 2008. As soon as demand picks up again, sales rise sharply. This is particularly the case for highly cyclical companies that are more exposed to swings in the economy than defensive stocks, which have more reliable and stable income streams. Moreover, the uptick in demand can feed on itself, as the economic recovery post the downturn gathers pace. Distributors, manufacturers and speciality chemical companies are key cyclical sectors where companies can quickly enter recovery and then move into an earnings upgrade cycle.

For instance, shares in European electronic components distributor Acal were trading 30 per cent below book value in early 2010 when I spotted their potential (*Investors Chronicle*, 'Bargain shares', 10 February 2010). Cash on the balance sheet accounted for half the share price and swift action by management to take costs out of the business in the previous year had returned it to profitability.

Driven by growth in the company's electronics order book, cost-cutting and margin improvement, revenues soared over the next year-and-a-half, and so did profits. Acal also used its cash pile sensibly and made a number of bolt-on acquisitions. Moreover, with underlying operating margins rising sharply from a cycle trough of around 2.5 per cent as the recovery took hold, then small increases in margins on rising sales had a dramatic impact on profits. It also helped drive Acal shares up by more than 140 per cent over the next 12 months.

■ **Changes in monetary and fiscal policy**. A good example of how this can alter the outlook for a whole industry are the changes in the UK government's housing policy, announced in the March 2013 Budget. By introducing a 'Help to buy' package of initiatives for UK homeowners, involving low-interest loans to mortgage customers, and a government guarantee on 20 per cent of the home loan, demand for housing is expected to rise as credit becomes more available to a wider group of potential homeowners.

However, unless the supply side changes, these initiatives will stoke house prices, which is good news for the country's housebuilders. In fact, with the major players reporting operating margins in the range of 8 to 12 per cent in their financial results in early 2013, even a modest 6 per cent rise in annual house prices would boost their operating profits between 50 and 75 per cent. That's because the extra revenue generated on these home sales would drop straight down to the bottom line, because it is being made on land already owned and in the pipeline for development.

Furthermore, the higher house prices rise, the higher margins will become, which will drive earnings up – assuming of course, that supply is held in check. In turn, this offers potential for the UK housebuilding sector to enter an earnings upgrade cycle.

■ **Exposure to the macro economy**. It is important to analyse where a company generates its sales as this will have a major implication for its ability to grow revenues and profits, and beat earnings expectations. That's why I always find out the revenue split to determine the exposure to end markets in geographic regions overseas that are enjoying strong economic growth.

■ **Legislative and structural changes.** A classic example of how structural and legislative change across industries can impact companies is illustrated by Norfolk-based Porvair, the only listed UK filtration business on the London stock market. The company makes fuel and coolant filters for most of the world's commercial aircraft – including Airbus and Boeing – whose robust order books have boosted demand for the company's products.

The industrial filter maker's technology is also used to make aircraft fuel tanks inert during refilling, by flooding empty tanks with nitrogen to negate sparks. Legislation has made such technology compulsory on new-build aircraft and is expected to be extended to older commercial planes.

Porvair also makes ceramic filters used to purify molten metals and clean more than half the global supply of aluminium each year. Demand for such filters has been buoyed by a move towards pricier and more environmentally friendly phosphate-free filters. So with legislative and structural changes buoying demand, Porvair has seen sales and profits soar over the past three years. Between mid-2010 and early 2013, the company issued no fewer than 14 consecutive trading statements that led to earnings upgrades. It also drove shares in the company up 300 per cent over a three-year period.

■ **Acquisitions.** When companies merge or announce major acquisitions management gives an indication of the cost savings or benefits from the deal. However, if the cost savings have been conservatively estimated in the first place, this offers potential for companies to surprise on the upside. In many cases, the board has multi-year targets in place to make a stated amount of cost savings. Therefore, if they can generate these savings earlier than expected, and keep restructuring costs in check, then it will underpin a cycle of rising profits above analyst expectations.

■ **Currency weakness.** Another major benefit of understanding where geographically a business generates its revenues is the impact this has on reported revenues and profits. That's because exchange rate movements have a bearing on the value of overseas earnings when they are translated back into the currency the company reports in.

Most companies do not hedge currency risk, so a major swing in the exchange rate can have a material impact on the sterling value of overseas earnings. A weaker currency helps demand for exports as a company's goods become cheaper overseas, assuming of course any increase in the imported input costs in the final product are not material.

■ **Outsourcing manufacturing.** In the previous decade, many businesses outsourced their manufacturing capabilities overseas in order to benefit from lower labour costs, and to boost operating margins and profits. Asia and Eastern Europe were the main beneficiaries of this mass export of labour from the UK.

True, many of the benefits of outsourcing have been offset by rising inflation in certain regions of the world and also by the weakness of sterling, which has made the cost of labour overseas more expensive for UK companies outsourcing their manufacturing. However it's still worth keeping an eye on UK companies with outsourced overseas operations, because once sterling's descent over the past five years (autumn of 2007 to spring of 2013) runs its course, then many companies could experience an earnings boost from cheaper outsourcing.

■ **Technological change.** The world's second largest company, Apple, is probably the best example of a business riding the earnings upgrade cycle as technology-hungry consumers show an insatiable appetite for its iPhones and iPads. From a standing start, the company took a fifth of the smartphone market between 2007 and 2011, replicating its dominance in the mobile music market built up since it launched iPods. Such market dominance has translated into a huge cash pile and earnings growth averaging 59 per cent a year between 2008 and 2012. It also led to a series of earnings upgrades from analysts, driving up the shares sevenfold between the final quarter of 2008 and the autumn of 2012.

Another good example of a company benefiting from changing consumer habits due to technological advances, and a much smaller one closer to home, is gaming operator Netplay TV. The company operates a number of interactive gaming services under an Alderney gaming licence, including Supercasino.com and Jackpot247.com.

These services can be viewed on Sky Channel 862, FIVE and ITV1. New customers are certainly tuning in as Netplay attracted almost 14,000 new depositing casino players in 2012 – a 51 per cent increase over the course of the year. Interestingly, the business is gaining traction with mobile and tablet players: this segment accounted for 31 per cent of all new deposits, a fourfold increase on the previous year.

Importantly, after factoring in higher marketing spend and TV advertising, which has been pulling in the new players, these customer acquisitions are proving highly profitable. Analysts upgraded earnings estimates by 16 per cent after bumper half-year figures in September 2012, and by a further 12 per cent following a trading statement in January 2013. Interestingly, the last upgrade in earnings was driven by a modest 4 per cent additional rise in revenues, reflecting the operational gearing of the business. The attractions of a modestly rated, cash-rich company in an earnings upgrade cycle also appealed to investors, which is one reason why the shares surged 50 per cent after my initial buy advice (*Investors Chronicle*, 'A share ready to hit the jackpot', 11 February 2013).

9

Follow the leader – director share deals

D irector share dealing in small-cap, fledgling and the lower end of the mid-cap companies is always worth investigating, for several reasons.

Firstly, if the insiders are using substantial amounts of their own resources to buy shares in their companies, it can be an amber signal that trading prospects are far better than outside investors think.

Secondly, when a number of directors are all buying at the same time and these transactions are not related to share option schemes, then the message is pretty clear: the board clearly believes that the company is being undervalued and aims to exploit the current share price in a big way.

Thirdly, share price movements in the small-cap segment of the stock market can be, by their nature, far more volatile than for larger caps, so if other investors follow the lead of the directors then this can have an accentuated impact on a company's subsequent share price performance.

Fourthly, it is far more difficult for directors of small-cap companies to take large positions in their companies than it is for the directors of larger caps, which are dominated by institutional trades in bargain sizes that run into millions of pounds. So when these insiders are staking large amounts of their own money, rather than just matching investments in share incentive schemes, it pays to find out why they have been buying in such large quantities, and whether there is an investment opportunity to exploit by following their lead. This is precisely why I always keep an eye out for interesting director deals.

Set some rules

Clearly, not all director share buys will make money, so it is worth setting some rules to weight the odds in your favour of making a profitable investment when following the lead of the insiders.

The first rule is that I rarely follow the lead of a main board director in a company that has just issued a profit warning. That's because, in most cases, the reason for the director buying is not necessarily because there is value in the shares, but rather it is a statement to the major shareholders that the director is committed to the company.

In effect, it is an insurance policy to prevent institutional shareholders, who have seen the value of their holdings significantly reduced following the profit warning, from demanding a change of leadership due to the management failure that led to the profit shortfall. For example, if a finance director or chief executive earning a basic salary of £250,000 decides to purchase shares in his company worth £50,000 post a profit warning, then this is only the equivalent of 10 weeks' gross salary. It would be an entirely different matter if the share purchase was equivalent to two-thirds, or even all, of the director's annual remuneration.

From my experience, the best investment gains are generally made by following directors of companies that display some of the following characteristics:

■ Earnings in upgrade cycles.

■ Early stages of recovery.

■ Potential to release upbeat news in forthcoming trading updates.

■ Director buying is made alongside a capital raising that materially improves the investment case.

That's because the insiders are ideally placed to see the early signs of an improvement in trading and the likely impact of changes in the order book, contract wins or benefits from acquisitions, they are backing with their own money.

Director selling is of less interest to me, because unless a director is disposing of a sizeable chunk of a shareholding, I view the selling as a way for directors to bank some of the gains earned on share option packages which form part of their remuneration.

To illustrate how the process of spotting the best director deals works in practice, and the key indicators that signal that the director buying is worth following, consider the following three case studies.

---

case study 19

Directors backing acquisitions with their own money

Stanley Gibbons may be the most famous name in stamps and a company that has been around for 155 years, but it is not stuck in some bygone age. In fact, in the first six months of 2012, the company's internet sales increased by 90 per cent to £1.3m, to account for 9 per cent of turnover. This is a market with huge potential as internet giant eBay's online stamp market is worth $268m (£172m).

Expanding online presence

So to tap into this area, Stanley Gibbons announced the acquisition of US-based online collectibles trading platform bidstart.com in early November 2012. Bidstart is mainly focused on the stamp and postcard market and has sold more than 3.5m items since inception. The real opportunity for Stanley Gibbons is to use its own expertise, brand, network and financial strength to create a much bigger collectibles trading platform for bidstart.

It was a sensibly priced deal too, with the initial consideration around £415,000 in cash and shares. Equally sensible, Stanley Gibbons raised £6m at 195p a share through a share placing to fund the purchase and investment in bidstart's technology, marketing and staff. The equity-raising also meant the company, which had a market value of £50m at the time, had the flexibility to pursue other growth opportunities in its own business.

Directors back the placing

Importantly, the directors of Stanley Gibbons were backing the fundraising. True, the dilution on EPS of the placing and the investment in bidstart meant that the company's profit and EPS growth would be held back in 2013; brokers only expected pre-tax profits to edge up from £5.5m to just £5.7m. However, this deal had the potential to transform the company's business model if it could make inroads into the online US stamp market. Moreover, the shares were modestly rated, priced on 12.5 times earnings estimates, which made them a relatively low-risk buying opportunity when I highlighted the investment case (*Investors Chronicle*, 'A stamp of authority', 5 November 2012).

It didn't take long for other investors to warm to the potential from the bidstart deal. Within three months, Stanley Gibbons' shares had risen 50 per cent to an all-time high of 295p.

Key lessons to learn:

■ Acquisition was low-risk and offered potential to transform the business.

■ Placing had institutional backing and widened the shareholder base.

■ Directors all bought in the placing, which showed signs of confidence.

■ Company was cash-rich post placing so ongoing investment in other parts of the business was not being hindered by the acquisition.

■ Modest earnings multiple provided scope for share price rerating once investors reappraised the investment case.

---

case study 20

Improvements in trading

The ninth largest UK car dealer by revenue, Vertu Motors, released an upbeat trading statement at its annual meeting in late July 2012. This revealed that since the financial year-end the company had posted like-for-like profit growth in each of the core areas of its business: new retail sales; used car sales; fleet and commercial sales; and vehicle servicing.

There was also a higher contribution to profits from dealerships acquired in the previous financial year. Overall, total revenues in the latest four-month trading period grew by 11.6 per cent, including like-for-like vehicle revenue growth of over 5 per cent. This update offered some reassurance to shareholders that, even in the face of a challenging consumer backdrop, Vertu would be able to at least maintain adjusted EPS at around 3p in the financial year to end-February 2013.

Directors have inside track

The directors obviously thought so too, and three of them splashed out over £40,000 buying shares in the company at a price of 28.25p following the trading update. It was easy to see why, because the shares were not only lowly rated on less than 10 times historic earnings, and offered a solid 2 per cent dividend yield, but they were priced on a huge 40 per cent discount to book value. That looked anomalous considering the company's solid asset backing, which included freehold property and a cash-rich balance sheet. The valuable sites alone were in the books for £83.8m, or 42p a share – 50 per cent more than Vertu's share price.

Taking the trading performance and sound fundamentals into consideration, I concluded that it was worth following the directors' lead and buying the shares at around 29.5p (*Investors Chronicle*, 'Vertu shares priced to motor', 9 August 2012).

Trading steps up a gear

The insiders buy signal proved spot on because the improvement in trading stepped up a gear over the next couple of months. In fact, by the time Vertu issued half-year results in October 2012, the board was able to report that the improving new car retail market had boosted like-for-like retail volume by 7.9 per cent. There was also an eye-catching 7.5 per cent growth in used car volumes.

Furthermore, pre-tax profit for the full year was expected to accelerate past analysts' previous estimates, prompting brokers to upgrade EPS forecasts by 7 per cent to 3.2p. And because the business is highly cash-generative, Vertu was able to splash out £7m on capital expenditure and acquisitions from operating cash flow alone. Shareholders also benefited and were rewarded with a 25 per cent hike in the interim dividend.

Shares move off the forecourt

There was more good news to come when Vertu announced a pre-close trading update in early March 2013. Like-for-like private new retail volumes had accelerated even more since the half-year stage, and buoyed by improving margins, full-year profits were now set to come in ahead of the upgraded earnings estimates. The company's shares motored on the news, hitting a high of 44p and provided investors who followed the directors' lead with a near 50 per cent share price gain in seven months.

Key lessons to learn:

■ Director buying added weight to the case that Vertu's improving sales performance had further to run.

■ Company undervalued on a sum-of-the parts basis with shares priced 40 per cent below book value.

■ Modest earnings multiple provided scope for share price rerating once investors reappraised the investment case.

■ Scope for earnings upgrades if sales momentum gathered speed.

■ Cash-rich balance sheet and strong operating cash flow offered potential for value-enhancing acquisitions and higher dividends.

---

case study 21

Director buying highlights catalysts for rerating

I was intrigued when I noticed that chairman Tony Hales of serviced office provider Workspace had splashed out £100,000 buying shares in his company in the autumn of 2010 (*Investors Chronicle*, 'Hot property', 4 October 2010).

Positive trading trends

On further investigation it was clear why, as the company had reported some positive trading trends. For instance, like-for-like occupancy rates at Workspace's properties had been rising, but not at the expense of rental income. The company was also adding value by refurbishing properties, a decision fully justified by an improvement in occupancy rates.

Interestingly, Workspace had just announced a smart looking deal to buy back £93m-worth of properties in 11 locations, from a joint venture from the beleaguered HBOS, for a bargain basement price of £75 per sq ft. There was undoubted scope to add value on several of these properties. For example, a site at Grand Union Centre, close to Ladbroke Grove in West London, had outline planning permission for 145 apartments and 110,000 sq ft of new commercial space. And in South London, the two-acre Wandsworth Business Village had planning approval for a major mixed-use scheme of 209 flats and a new 80,000 sq ft business centre.

Well funded

Workspace had no funding worries, having refinanced a £200m five-year debt facility with Nationwide, Santander and BayernLB, and a £150m facility with RBS was not due for repayment for another two years. In total, the company had £383m of debt secured on £725m-worth of properties, to give a modest loan-to-value ratio of 53 per cent. Untapped credit facilities of £31m provided further headroom for the company.

Trading below book value

Despite the potential to generate significant capital upside for shareholders from those property developments, Workspace's shares were trading 17 per cent below the company's last reported net asset value and 20 per cent below forecasts for the March 2011 financial year-end. In effect, the market value and total debt of the company – the enterprise value – was below the replacement cost of the assets owned.

Shareholders also received a healthy annual payout, funded from stable rental income, which gave a 3.5 per cent dividend yield on the shares.

Positive newsflow

Mr Hales' lead was well worth following because within six months the company had agreed a deal with specialist London residential developer Mount Anvil for the regeneration of Wandsworth Business Village; received planning consent for 557 apartments and a new 60,000 sq ft business centre at the company's Bow Enterprise Industrial Estate, close to the Olympic Park; and entered into a five-year joint venture with BlackRock UK Property Fund to target high-yielding multi-let industrial and office buildings in London and the south-east.

Given this upbeat newsflow, it was not surprising that shares in Workspace were making headway. In fact, by the time I advised banking profits they had risen 30 per cent in only seven months (*Investors Chronicle*, 'A level playing field', 16 May 2011).

Key lessons to learn:

- Improving trading performance.

- Potential for newsflow from a number of developments.

- Well financed and no funding concerns.

- Shares trading below replacement cost of properties on balance sheet and well below book value.

- Decent dividend funded from cash flow from rents on developments.

10

Technical analysis

As part of my investment analysis I always have a close look at technical indicators. A company may tick all the right boxes by offering a decent potential return based on traditional valuation techniques, but if the chart is telling you something different then this should raise alarm bells.

In order to identify shares that have a positive set-up on their charts, and to avoid the ones where the technical situation is unfavourable, I use a number of tried and tested systems to determine whether recommending an investment in a company is warranted.

Momentum indicators

The key indicators I use to identify key turning points for share prices are momentum and the relative strength indicators (RSI). The most useful of these is the 14-day RSI, which is available on most charting software programmes. Developed by J. Welles Wilder, the RSI is a momentum oscillator that measures the speed and change of price movements. It oscillates between zero and 100 and is considered overbought when the reading is above 70, and oversold when below 30. Signals can also be generated by looking for divergences, where a company's share price continues to rise and reach fresh highs but the RSI doesn't. This is known as negative divergence and can prelude a share price sell-off as the momentum driving the share price higher starts to wane.

At the other extreme, when a company's share price has been stuck in a downward trend, what I am looking for is positive divergence. This is where the price makes new lows, but the RSI reading doesn't. When the RSI reading is at extreme oversold levels – in the 20 to 30 range – and is not confirming the sell-off, this is a good indicator that a snap-back rally, or start of a multi-week recovery could be close. When this happens, the selling pressure abates and buyers who had been sitting on the sidelines come in to snap up a bargain.

The RSI readings can also be used in conjunction with key signals on the daily and weekly candlestick charts to identify key turning points.

Key day reversals, hammer tops and hammer bottoms

Alarm bells should start ringing when a share consecutively hits higher daily closing prices, but then fails to close higher the next trading day and dips below the previous high. This is known as a key day reversal (KDR) and can often signify the start of a short-term downward trend if the RSI is in overbought territory. When the reversal occurs on the weekly candlestick chart, this increases the risk of a multi-week share price decline.

Another warning signal of a share price reversal is a hammer top. This is when the share price hits another intra-day high following a strong up-move, only for profit-taking to set in, and the price to fall back to the previous day's close. Volume levels can spike at this point, way above the normal daily average, as a war of attrition takes place between new buyers arriving just as the party is ending, and existing investors, who are sitting on gains, leaving the dance floor before the music stops. The shares then have a tendency to fall back, retracing previous gains.

The reverse of a hammer top is a hammer bottom, which occurs when shares are oversold based on the RSI reading and primed for a bounce. After a series of closing lows, the share price reaches another intra-day low, but buyers come in to take the closing price back to the prior day's close. So instead of blindly trying to catch a falling knife, it is well worth waiting for this signal because hammer bottoms are very reliable in identifying turning points on the charts when there is positive divergence.

It's worth noting that oversold shares can stay oversold for lengthy periods of time as the price trends endlessly lower. That's why using hammer bottoms, KDRs and RSI readings to time your entry point, and so avoid buying into downtrends too early, are by far some of the most reliable techniques around.

Chart break-outs

Some of my share recommendations in *Investors Chronicle* have enjoyed explosive price moves following publication of my articles. That's partly as a result of trading volumes increasing dramatically as other like-minded investors concur that the investment case is sound and the shares are worth buying.

But it's also because I target companies that have either just given, or are on the cusp of giving, a major share price break-out on their point-and-figure charts. This type of chart consists of columns of Xs (showing price rises) and Os (showing price falls) arranged on a square grid. When a company's share price increases, a rising column of black Xs is created – a rally. When the index falls, a descending column of red Os appears – a decline. What I do is quite simple: I screen company charts for situations where the next move is a break-out above the last high from the previous share price rally, or where the price move would create a break-out above a previous intermediate high, dating back months, or even years. When this point-and-figure break-out occurs, it can signal the start of a major price move.

It's not difficult to do, as I use a charting package to check at the close of trading each day for point-and-figure break-outs on all the companies listed on the London stock market. There are a large number of companies offering this service and the one I use is from Investors Intelligence (www.investorsintelligence.com).

By the same token, I avoid companies that have given point-and-figure sell signals on their charts. This is when the last break-out is a column of Os going lower than the previous column of Os and no buy signal (no column of Xs breaking above the previous column of Xs) has happened since the sell signal.

Spikes in trading volumes

Volume is the rocket fuel of the market, so for a share price break-out to be the real deal, and the start of a multi-week rally, trading volumes need to confirm the price move. In other words, for the move to be genuine and not reverse shortly thereafter, it has to be driven by a rise in buying activity and greater investor participation. This mitigates the risk that the break-out will turn out to be false and a 'bull trap'.

12-month highs and lows

I also screen for shares in companies showing positive momentum. One way is to target share prices hitting multi-week highs where the RSI is not overbought and trading volume is confirming the price move. This improves the odds of the share price continuing to run up further, assuming of course that the investment case still backs up the price move.

Share prices hitting 12-month lows are also of interest because these flag up companies to put on your watch list for when the RSI enters oversold territory and there is positive divergence on the chart.

Exploit stock overhangs

Websites offering streaming real-time prices and Level II quotes put retail investors on a level playing field with professional traders in the City, meaning they are better placed to exploit stock overhangs. Sometimes, especially after some positive company-specific newsflow, buying activity increases, but a company's offer price refuses to budge as market makers clear the decks by unloading stock held on their books to new buyers.

For investors, the key is to buy in just before the overhang is about to clear and the share price responds to the increased buying pressure. Unfortunately, this is the great unknown since no-one, apart from the individual market maker, knows how much stock has to be cleared before a share price will start to run away.

Sometimes it can only take a matter of hours, but in other cases it may take several weeks before the overhang clears or a persistent seller disappears.

Fortunately help is at hand. The first tell-tale sign is when the bid-offer spread narrows dramatically as market makers start to run out of stock and are bidding in sellers at ever-increasing prices. The streaming real-time prices of trades going through the market will indicate the narrowing of the spread, as will Level II prices on the order book. While this is going on, market makers may increasingly trade stock between themselves. Finally, when the overhang clears, there will be a break-out as the first market maker is forced to raise his offer price.

---

case study 22

Clearing stock overhangs ahead of a price move

To see how this works in practice consider the trading activity in shares of Oakley Capital Investments, a closed-end Aim-traded investment company I recommended buying in early 2013 (*Investors Chronicle*, 'Bargain shares for 2013', 8 February 2013).

Investors were set to hear good news when Oakley reported full-year results in April 2013. That's because the company, which takes stakes in private equity ventures and provides mezzanine debt finance, had sold one of its major holdings: Emesa, an online consumer auction and booking platform for the leisure sector. Oakley owned a 68 per cent equity stake in that business and had just announced that it would book a hefty 21 per cent uplift (around £4.5m) on the carrying value of its £21.1m investment. That represented a chunky sum of money for a company with a market value of £176m. So, with Oakley shares offered in the market at 140p, the company was being valued on a hefty 22 per cent discount to its net asset value of around 180p.

That discount looked unwarranted when you consider that, post the disposal, Oakley was sitting on 77p a share of net cash (before factoring in any other transactions yet to be reported at the time). Strip this amount from the 140p share price and Oakley's other investments – worth 103p a share – were being valued in the share price at a bargain basement 63p, despite their obvious potential to produce capital gains.

Readers of *Investors Chronicle* clearly liked the investment case and over 2m shares were traded over the four days following my article. That represented 1.6 per cent of the issued share capital, so trading volumes were high. However, despite the heavy buying in Oakley's shares, the price hardly budged due to a stock overhang. That was until the fifth trading day when the company's share price surged by 5 per cent, as the overhang cleared and market makers had run out of stock.

With market makers now holding low levels of stock on their books, Oakley's share price continued to tick up over the next three weeks on modest buying. Within a month the price had risen 14 per cent.

Key lessons to learn:

■ Catalysts were in place for the share price discount to book value to narrow, but Oakley's share price was being held back by a stock overhang.

■ The first sign that the overhang was starting to clear was the small rise in Oakley's share price after three days of heavy buying. With market makers now holding low levels of stock on their books, and more investors attracted by the investment case (having taken time to do their own research), the net result was a multi-week rerating of the shares.

11

Assessing risk

n previous chapters I have focused on how to uncover undervalued
companies that should provide scope for share price appreciation as,
and when, other investors acknowledge the investment case.

However, it is important to be aware of the risk embedded in a company's
valuation, as any two companies will have a different risk profile. The aim
is to maximise the return available on your capital by taking as little risk as
possible. In order to do this, I carry out 16 different risk assessments on every
company I analyse, in order to get a picture of the level of investment risk.
A company has to pass at least 10 of these tests to make my shortlist.

■ Management track record

To ascertain the quality of a management team I always look at a
company's annual report and accounts to view the history of the board
members. I take into account their length of service – the longer the better;
roles undertaken at previous employers and the degree of success in these
positions; and assess the level of corporate governance.

One company that scores well here is FTSE 250 precision engineer
Renishaw. The five main board members have an average of 30 years
service each, and there are three non-executive directors sitting on the
board. All the main board have significant experience in the company's
field of expertise, which is reflected in the impressive performance of the
businesses the company runs. It is also one reason why Renishaw's share

price enjoys a premium rating of around 18 times forward earnings – well in excess of the market and sector averages. The shares have proved a good investment, rising ninefold between the start of 2009 and early 2013.

■ Succession risk

When a founder or chief executive has been the driving force behind a company for many years, it raises questions as to how the business will cope once the director steps down. Moreover, when this change of management at the top happens, it can signify the point at which the growth story is starting to lose its appeal. I am wary of companies where the succession risk is too great.

For instance, shares in the UK's largest supermarket chain, Tesco, rose by more than 300 per cent in the 13 years under the leadership of Terry Leahy, who became chief executive in 1997. Mr Leahy's appointment followed the retirement of his mentor, Lord MacLaurin, and coincided with Tesco's major push into overseas markets. However, shares in the food retailer have performed poorly since June 2010 when Mr Leahy announced his intention to step down. In fact, in the two years since his departure in March 2011, they have actually fallen in value and the company even warned on profits in 2012. The retailer also reported a sharp 13 per cent decline in trading profit in the financial year ending February 2013.

■ Shareholding structure

It's always worth finding out whether a company is being run for the benefit of outside shareholders, or for the benefit of a small number of large shareholders who are main board directors. This can create a major conflict of interest where the minority of shareholders have little influence over how the company operates.

That's not to say that companies where the main board controls over 50 per cent of the issued share capital don't offer attractive investment opportunities. Clearly many do, as is shown in the case of Mountview Estates, a residential property company in which major shareholders and the founding Sinclair family control more than two-thirds of the shares in issue.

case study 23

Analysing the share structure

Mountview holds investments in three areas: regulated tenancies; ground rent units and life tenancies on a portfolio of properties, mainly based in London and the south-east. There is no doubt its business model has stood the test of time, having been incorporated in 1937.

A couple of decades later, the company obtained a full quote on the London Stock Exchange when the shares were sold for eleven shillings, or 55p. Adjust for subsequent share splits and scrip issues, and that equates to a share price of 11p; which means that in the past 52 years Mountview's share price has risen over 500-fold to a high of 5,780p by late April 2013. There have also been substantial dividends paid to shareholders funded through the rents received.

Importantly, it's a rising stream of dividend income that differentiates Mountview from other companies dominated by sizeable family holdings. That's because the board has a vested interest in raising the payout, as this benefits the controlling shareholders and, for some directors, represents the majority of their income from the company.

With Mountview generating annual earnings of around 500p a share, and paying out a dividend of 165p a share, the difference of 335p is boosting the company's net asset value. That is one of the reasons why Mountview reported a 7 per cent increase in book value to 5,971p a share in the six months to end-September 2012. Moreover, if the company put in a similar performance in the second half of its financial year ending March 2013, book value would rise to around 6,200p a share at the period-end.

The solid income stream, funded through rents on properties, and the ability of the company to grow net asset value through retained profits from rents received, were the main reasons why I recommended buying shares in Mountview at around 5,000p in early 2013 (*Investors Chronicle*, 'Chart break-out for solid income play', 12 February 2013). The price subsequently rose 15 per cent in the following two months to sharply narrow the share price discount to net asset value, as other like-minded investors also noted the anomalous valuation I had identified.

By the same token, I generally avoid non-income-paying small-cap and Aim-traded companies with market values below £10m, where the board is dominated by founding shareholders. Their interests may not be aligned with those of outside investors and institutional shareholders have little power to force changes on the company due to their relatively low shareholdings.

■ Net asset value growth per share

On most corporate websites there is a breakdown of the financial performance of the company over a five-year period. However, with a little time and effort you can go back even further to build up a track record of the long-term performance of profits, earnings and dividends. You can also find out how much value the company has added over the years by calculating the growth in net asset value per share.

I use this figure instead of changes in total shareholder funds, since the latter can be boosted by share issues, whereas net asset value per share adjusts for these and is a far better reflection of how much profit has been retained by the company after paying out dividends.

case study 24

Analyse dividend and net asset value per share growth rates

Consider the case of Sheffield-based construction and property company Henry Boot. Shares in the company were trading around 10 per cent below book value when I highlighted the investment case at the end of 2012 (*Investors Chronicle*, 'Rerating beckons', 12 November 2012).

They were also priced 20 per cent below my conservative sum-of-the-parts valuation, even though Henry Boot has proved to be a quality company with a fantastic track record of growing shareholder value and rewarding loyal investors. The board had more than trebled the dividend in the past 18 years, and raised net asset value per share by an average of 6 per cent a year in this time. That's after factoring in dividend payments. Admittedly, the payout had been cut post the financial crisis, but importantly the company had "set a target of building the dividend back to the pre-recession level of 5p per share, as market conditions allow".

Despite these positives, shares in the asset-backed company could be purchased for 124p at the end of 2012, so the prospective dividend yield at the time was almost 4 per cent. Four months later and Henry Boot's shares had enjoyed a 40 per cent rerating as other investors cottoned on to the anomalous valuation.

Table 11.1   Henry Boot's impressive financial performance (1994 to 2012)

Year to 31 Dec	Pre-tax profit (£m)	Dividend per share (p)	Net asset value per share (p)
1994	8.2	1.4	37
1995	8.7	1.5	40
1996	9.4	1.6	43
1997	10.1	1.7	44
1998	10.6	1.8	47
1999	11.2	2.0	51
2000	12.2	2.2	58
2001	13.4	2.4	63
2002	17.1	2.7	72
2003	30.0	3.0	89
2004	23.2	3.3	84
2005	30.2	3.8	94
2006	40.8	4.4	116
2007	46.5	5.0	139
2008	19.3	5.0	146
2009	-11.9	2.5	135
2010	18.9	3.5	145
2011	16.1	4.3	142
2012	13.9	4.7	138

Source: *Investors Chronicle*, 'Rerating beckons', 12 November 2012

■ **Profit warnings risk**

As a rule I tend to avoid companies that have warned on profits a number of times in recent years; for two good reasons. Firstly, it raises serious questions about the competency of management and the controls in place within the business. Secondly, if a company has warned on profits, history proves that the risk of it doing so again is far greater.

■ **Acquisition risk**

Not all acquisitions create value and I am wary of buying shares in companies that have been on a massive spending spree, funded by issuing new shares like confetti.

That's because vendors of the acquired companies will understandably want to get their cash out at some stage; and this can create a stock overhang. There is also the issue of deferred consideration for these acquisitions, based on earn-out agreements, which can lead to even more shares being issued to vendors at a later date. As a result, shares in companies that have made several acquisitions may appear to offer value by being lower rated than peers, but more often than not this is a 'value trap'.

That's because the sub-sector rating reflects the greater risk of a subdued share price performance due to: a potential stock overhang from the vendor holdings, and dilution to existing shareholders resulting from the issue of additional shares to meet earn-out obligations.

■ **Legislation and geopolitical risk**

Government intervention varies widely across different industries, and in the most extreme cases, can lead to re-nationalisation of companies at the expense of private shareholders as former shareholders in Railtrack plc will know all too well.

The group was placed into railway administration under the Railways Act 1993 in October 2001, following an application to the High Court by the then Transport Secretary, Stephen Byers. Railtrack's financial problems came to light after the company incurred huge compensation claims in the aftermath of the Hatfield rail crash, at a time when it was also funding the costs of modernising the West Coast Main Line.

There are many cases too of large corporations suffering due to government intervention overseas. In April 2012, Argentina sent shock waves through the oil industry by announcing plans to re-nationalise the local oil assets of YPF, the country's largest oil producer, from the Spanish firm Repsol, which had held a majority stake in YPF since 1999.

It is therefore a good discipline when evaluating companies to consider the geopolitical risk and decide whether this has potential to pose a significant risk. This is why the earnings of oil producers and miners operating in certain regions of Russia, Africa and the Middle East are generally valued less richly than similar companies operating in more stable Western markets.

■ Pricing power

The ability of companies to pass on higher input prices varies enormously across industries. Companies in regulated sectors, such as water utilities and transport operators, are more restricted in their ability to raise prices since the government regulator factors in the cost inflation and investment needs of these companies into the regulated price framework.

In the oil industry companies can hedge their exposure by forward selling production, but the oil producer's profits are largely determined by market forces, which are ultimately dependent on global economic growth and the demand this creates for energy.

Companies with unique technology, or where barriers to entry are high and there are a limited number of operators in the field, offer the greatest pricing power. That's because end users have little choice but to accept price rises due to limited alternatives. Pricing power is by far weakest in commoditised industries, which is why distributors trade on relatively low earnings multiples.

■ Currency risk

Most companies do not hedge their overseas earnings against exchange rate fluctuations, so when these international sales are translated back into the currency a company reports in it can have a major bearing on financial results.

It is imperative to find out where in the world a company generates its sales, and the likely growth expected from these regions. That's especially the case since the start of the financial crisis in 2007, whereupon many UK companies have benefited from improved international sales. This is due to the more competitive price of UK-sourced goods, reflecting the heavy falls in sterling against the currencies of the UK's major trading partners since the start of the crisis.

It also means that ongoing weakness in sterling has a positive impact on the reported sales and profits earned on goods sold overseas where contract prices have been fixed in the overseas currency. Clearly, when sterling is strong, this can work against export companies due to declines in sterling-denominated revenues and the margin earned on fixed-price overseas contracts.

■ Interest rate cycles

The interest rate cycle has a major bearing on valuations of different sectors of the stock market. For instance, high-growth technology companies are likely to be valued on the 'net present value' of their future cash flows. To calculate this, cash flow projections are discounted back into present day values by applying a discount rate to them. The higher the rate applied, the lower the value of a cash flow when it is discounted. Due to the compounding effect, this means the further you project, the less valuable the cash flows become in 'net present value' terms in a rising interest rate environment.

It also explains why technology stocks performed so incredibly well in the early stages of the bull market that started in March 2009 – within a year of hitting its bear market low, the Nasdaq 100 index had doubled in value in the US. That's because, with interest rates slashed by central banks, and yields falling for medium and longer dated government bonds, the discount rate applied to both the cash flow and profit estimates of these companies was much lower. In turn, the net present value of the discounted profit and cash flow estimates increased. So not only did these technology companies receive a lift from an improving economic outlook, but also from unconventional monetary policy.

It's well worth considering how a company is being valued in times of unconventional monetary policy and ultra-low interest rates, and whether it will be valued any differently when financial stimulus is withdrawn by the major central banks and more traditional monetary policy is adopted. The greater the difference between the two valuations, the greater the risk.

▪ Index tracking risk

Every three months the FTSE International Committee meets to make quarterly changes to the FTSE 100 and FTSE 250 indices in the UK, with the laggards dropping out of the blue-chip index and being replaced by the largest companies from the mid-cap index. This meeting happens on the second Wednesday of March, June, September and December.

Around this time, companies likely to be promoted to the FTSE 100 – based on their market value meeting the criteria set out by the FTSE International Committee – see technical buying from index-tracking fund managers re-weighting their portfolios. There is also buying from traders exploiting the opportunity to make money from these index changes. Companies dropping out of the index not surprisingly come under selling pressure.

These changes also have implications for movements in the FTSE Small Cap and FTSE Fledgling indices. Once a year, in early December, the FTSE International Committee reassesses the constituents of these indices based on the market value of the companies at the time.

As a result, it is worth considering the likelihood of technical buying around the time of the index reviews. In particular, try to assess the downside risk of a company dropping out of a particular index and the potential for share price gains for companies likely to be promoted.

▪ Peer group premium risk

Some companies enjoy significant premium ratings based on their PE ratio relative to their peer group. That can be wholly justified by the track record of the company over a number of years, the quality of earnings and the earnings growth predicted.

However there comes a point when the premium rating, both relative to the market and peers, leaves no room for manoeuvre if trading disappoints. The obvious risk is that any contraction in the earnings multiple from an elevated level can lead to a very sharp de-rating of a share price. If this risk is too high I simply avoid the shares.

It is therefore important to quantify how much of the current earnings multiple is in effect a premium rating above peers, some or all of which would disappear, if the company fails to meet investors' lofty expectations.

---

case study 25

Handbags at dawn

This is exactly what happened to shares in Mulberry, which had risen 44-fold in the three years between June 2009 and the summer of 2012, valuing the maker of luxury handbags at £1.5bn.

To put this eye-watering valuation into perspective, the company only made pre-tax profits of £36m in the financial year to March 2012. Investors had chased the shares so high they were trading on 57 times post-tax earnings – more than double the rating of Mulberry's international peer group, which included the luxury brands Burberry, Gucci and Prada.

Even if Mulberry managed to double net profits every two years out to 2016, which would be quite some feat, it was still trading on 14 times 2016 earnings estimates. In other words, the share price premium to peers was so large, and the earnings growth expectations were so high, that if the company even slightly missed earnings guidance its shares would tumble.

That's exactly what happened, as the combination of weak trading in Asia, and a drop in tourist traffic in London, led to Mulberry issuing a major profit warning in March 2013. Instead of making profits of £46m in the financial year – as analysts had forecast when the shares were riding an all-time high in the summer of 2012 – Mulberry would now only deliver profits of £26m, much less than the previous year. To compound matters, and reflecting the poor trading backdrop, investors now valued these profits at a much lower earnings multiple. Mulberry shares crashed.

■ **Liquidity risk**

As a rule I try to focus only on companies trading on a bid-offer spread of less than 2 per cent, otherwise dealing costs are creating a massive hurdle to overcome before an investment turns a profit. It's for this reason that I hardly ever advise buying shares when the spread widens above 4-5 per cent. But if I do, the investment upside potential has to be so substantial that it more than compensates for the initial loss of capital from the higher dealing costs incurred.

I also look at the past trading volumes to see whether it's possible to deal in a reasonable bargain size, both for buy and sell orders, and check the normal market size in the shares on the London Stock Exchange website. This is the minimum amount of stock a market maker has to deal in if requested. Finally, I try to monitor trades going through the market to see whether the spread widens materially intra-day from the one quoted by brokers.

■ **Volatility risk**

There is a huge difference between making a 10 or 15 per cent gain on an investment when the share price trends up in small daily moves, than on one characterised by wild swings in both directions. Higher share price volatility increases investment risk as the downside to your capital is far greater. So to compensate, you need a much higher return.

■ **Share price beta**

Some of the companies I recommend have a very low beta relative to their underlying benchmark index, which means that fluctuations in the general market have little impact on the share prices. This works both ways. In a strong uptrend you really don't want to be holding a share that fails to benefit from more buoyant investor sentiment. But equally in downtrends, holding shares in a company that doesn't track the market lower is a far more defensive option.

■ **Economic risk**

At certain times of the year, certain sectors perform much better than others, which I will discuss in more detail in the next chapter. It's worth noting that growth or cyclical sectors have historically done well in the winter months. That's because the winter creates economic risks, and to compensate for these, investors can expect higher returns from shares. The reverse is true in the summer, when shares in defensive sectors have performed best.

12

Market trends

A major consideration in making any investment decision is to understand how historic market trends impact sector performances. A company may appear undervalued based on fundamental investment analysis, and the chart set-up may be relatively positive, but investing in the wrong sector at the wrong time of the year is like running up a down escalator. It makes it incredibly difficult to generate a positive outcome.

Therefore, it is imperative to understand how the equity market, and sectors within it perform at different times of the year. This will avoid the sector headwinds the stock market blows in the direction of investors, and help you ride the tailwinds to maximise investment gains.

Historic market trends

In the past 47 years, the FTSE All-Share index – which is comprised of around 600 companies in the FTSE 100, FTSE 250 and FTSE SmallCap indices – has produced a woeful return of 1.8 per cent between the end of April and Halloween. *Investors Chronicle's* brilliant economist Chris Dillow has highlighted this long-term trend a number of times in the past (*Investors Chronicle*, 'Make 34 per cent from four phone calls', 8 July 2005; and *Investors Chronicle*, 'Pumpkins, chickens and volatility', 27 April 2010). The UK market has fallen in no fewer than 16 of these 47 years. That creates an almighty headwind for investors attempting to post positive returns in this particular six-month period.

To put this into perspective, the average return on the FTSE All-Share index in the period between Halloween and May Day has been more than 13 per cent since 1965. Furthermore, the risk of losing money over the winter and spring is much lower because in only seven of those 47 years did the UK stock market actually fall in that period (*Investors Chronicle*, 'Why not invest seasonally', 30 April 2012). In fact, the market has risen 85 per cent of the time over the winter and spring, which has led to a benign tailwind for investors in equity markets.

It's worth noting that the trend for the market to underperform over the summer doesn't work all the time; there have been no fewer than 13 summers in the past 47 years when the UK stock market has risen between the end of April and start of November. The last was in 2012, when the FTSE All-Share index posted a 2.4 per cent return. That said, even when the market does rise over the summer, expect the potential for some volatile trading. For instance, between the start of May and early June 2012 the index fell by around 10 per cent as eurozone worries came to the fore and spooked investors.

And when equity markets post absolute falls in this six-month period, they can really tumble. In 2011, it was the threat of the US defaulting on its debt mountain, and further eruptions in the European sovereign debt markets, that sent the market spiralling down a stomach-churning 21 per cent between the start of May and early August. In 2010, investors trying to make money from equities were anchored by a 17 per cent drop in the markets between the end of April and late June.

Even in 2009, when the markets powered up 20 per cent over the summer and into the autumn, investors had to first endure a sell-off – albeit a modest one at only 3 per cent – before the rally resumed. It was a similar story in May 2006 when the FTSE All-Share index sold off almost 10 per cent within a month before resuming its bull trend.

Understanding how markets behave

It is relatively easy to understand why equities perform in this way. It's because, after such a stellar performance over the winter and spring months, investors have a habit of becoming too complacent. This is given more substance once you consider that three of the best performing months of the year fall in this six-month period: April (which has produced an average monthly return of 3.1 per cent since 1965); January (3.0 per cent) and December (2.6 per cent). As a result, share prices run ahead of themselves by late April, which increases the potential for a sharp sell-off on any spike in risk aversion.

A smarter way to play the markets

True, investors could just ditch their equity holdings in late April, with a view to reinvesting in the final quarter of the year to take advantage of the more favourable market conditions. However, being out of equities completely is a risky business, especially in bull markets, as the experience of 2009 clearly shows.

Fortunately there is a smart way to play the historically less benign equity markets between the end of April and October that mitigates the risk of losing money: rotate investments between sectors. Different sectors perform differently at various times of the year, as Chris Dillow has demonstrated (*Investors Chronicle*, 'Five seasonal trading strategies', 15 December 2006). The bumper market returns produced over the winter and spring are largely generated by cyclical or value sectors, whereas in the summer defensive sectors do best.

As a result, a policy of reweighting portfolios out of cyclical companies into more defensive holdings over the summer has historically paid dividends. This means that you still have exposure to benefit from a general market rise, which lifts all boats, but also have a bias towards the sectors that have historically performed well against the market at this time of year. Chris Dillow has shown that the main defensive sectors to focus on are: utilities (water and electricity companies); pharmaceuticals; beverages and tobacco (*Investors Chronicle*, 'Make 34 per cent from four phone calls', 8 July 2005).

The opposite is true in the winter months, when you want more exposure from the fourth quarter onwards to shares in more cyclical sectors, and less exposure to those in defensive sectors. Chris Dillow explains that the main cyclical sectors to focus on are technology; computer software; electronics and telecoms (*Investors Chronicle*, 'Make 26 per cent the easy way', 1 June 2007). In the first quarter of the year, the standing dish is the construction sector and housebuilders in particular (*Investors Chronicle*, 'Five seasonal trading strategies', 15 December 2006; and *Investors Chronicle*, 'How to bank a fortune', *23 June 2006).*

Create watchlists

The other obvious investment strategy is to create watchlists of your favourite shares with a view to trying to pick up a bargain in the summer if risk aversion rises, and the stock market takes a tumble. If this happens, the most heavily oversold shares will undoubtedly be in cyclical sectors. So by biding your time and playing a waiting game over the summer, you could manage to buy cyclical shares at their low point of the year and on relatively attractive valuations. In a few months' time, other investors may once again be looking to increase their exposure to these cyclical shares, but at a price higher than you may have paid.

Dash for trash

Regular readers of *Investors Chronicle* will know that I have a strong interest in the small-cap segment of the stock market. All the companies I highlight are good-quality businesses, and are undervalued based on sound tried and tested investment techniques, which in time have uncovered companies with the potential to enjoy a share price rerating.

However, I have noted that a certain segment of small-cap companies perform very well between late November and the end of January. These companies all have one thing in common: they have proved a disastrous investment over the previous few years, and as a result, their share prices are at multi-year lows.

I call it a 'dash for trash', whereby some investors playing the markets in the benign and highly profitable months of December and January are willing to take on more risk and buy into these bombed-out small-caps. It is a high-risk strategy, because the reason for the rise in the share prices of these minnows has very little to do with an improvement in the trading outlook and operational performance of the companies concerned. It has all to do with an improving appetite for risk. As soon as this appetite starts to wane, shares in these companies can be expected to lose some, or in many cases the vast majority, of the gains racked up over this specific two-month period.

That said, this 'dash for trash' phenomenon does offer a short-term investment opportunity to buy a small number of these bombed-out minnows in late November, with the intention of riding the habitual Christmas rally in equities into the New Year.

Capitalise on small-cap outperformance

Historically the small-cap segment of the market performs generally well during the winter months. This can be attributed to two main factors: liquidity and the perception that small-cap companies are riskier.

If investors are less risk averse at this time of year, and with a seasonal investment tailwind behind the market during the benign months of December and January, the conditions are in place for small-caps to perform well. It really doesn't take much to get share prices in some of these small-cap companies moving. When they do, there is scope for outperformance of the mid- and large-caps.

There are technical reasons too, for the strong performance of small-caps. In particular, trading volumes on the London Stock Exchange in the latter part of December and into early January have historically been well below the average of the year. This is because this window coincides with a traditional two-week holiday period when market participants are more likely to head off for a well-earned break. Trading volumes drop and share prices can move up sharply on low volumes. Since small-cap shares are less liquid to trade than mid-caps and blue-chips, this makes them more volatile and more prone to sharp price moves on relatively low trading volumes (*Investors Chronicle*, 'Stock market mastermind', 22 July 2005).

A strategy of rotating investments into small-caps and more cyclical companies can accentuate returns in the nine-week trading period between the start of December and the end of January. This is one of the reasons that the 24 recommendations I gave in *Investors Chronicle* in the final quarter of 2012 performed so well, rising by an average of 16.6 per cent on an offer-to-bid basis when I reviewed them in early January 2013 (*Investors Chronicle*, 'Stock-picking marvels', 16 January 2013). That's because 20 of the 24 recommendations were small-cap shares, almost all of which were in cyclical sectors. This performance compares favourably with a 2 per cent rise in the FTSE All-Share index in the final quarter of 2012 and the 5.8 per cent rise in the FTSE SmallCap index in the same period.

A good example of how this can generate bumper returns was my recommendation to buy shares in East London housebuilder Telford Homes (*Investors Chronicle*, 'Gold winning performance', 23 October 2012).

---

case study 26

Cyclical small-cap investing

I had selected shares in Telford Homes as one of my bargain share picks of 2012 (*Investors Chronicle*, 'Bargain shares', 10 February 2012). Eight months later and the company's share price had already risen by 50 per cent. However all the ingredients were in place for a spectacular rerating of the same order in a very short period of time.

In a pre-close trading statement ahead of half-year results on 28 November 2012, Telford had turned in an Olympic-winning per-formance, having sold 85 per cent of its targeted completions for the financial year ending 31 March 2013. First-half sales more than doubled to 252 units, and with margins up considerably, the company was set to deliver a spectacular set of results in five weeks' time. It also meant that full-year earnings estimates were in the bag, as Telford only needed to sell another 42 homes by March 2013 to hit Shore Capital's full-year pre-tax profit estimate of £8m, up from £3m in the previous year.

The medium-term outlook was also promising, as Telford had secured a further 218 sales on its developments in the past six months, mainly driven by demand from overseas investors attracted to the decent rental yields on offer – as much as 6 per cent on some units; high tenant demand and the safe-haven status of London property. As a result, the financial performance for the year to March 2014 was now expected to exceed previous guidance, forcing analysts to upgrade their pre-tax profit estimates of £10m.

In other words, the company was set to more than treble, or potentially quadruple profits, over a two-year period. However Telford's share price failed to reflect this fact, trading around historic book value, rated on less than 10 times forward earnings and offering a prospective yield of 3 per cent. Within three months, Telford's share price had risen a further 50 per cent and had more than doubled in less than a year.

Key lessons to learn:

■ Telford is a small-cap company in a cyclical sector and was entering into a benign period where both small-caps and cyclical stocks performed strongly.

■ Investors had yet to fully recognise potential for earnings upgrades.

■ Shares in housebuilders do well in the first quarter of the year. This increases the odds of some investors 'jumping the gun' by buying early ahead of 1 January in anticipation of making gains in the first three months of the year.

■ Strong demand for London property meant Telford's potential to boost profits from rising house prices was greater than any other listed UK housebuilder. In fact when the company released a pre-close trading statement in mid-April 2013, it confirmed that the selling prices achieved were ahead of expectations. And with contracts exchanged for the sale of a record 803 open market properties in the 12 months to end March 2013, representing a 74 per cent rise in sales on the previous financial year, pre-tax profits had beaten analyst estimates. This news sent shares in the company soaring to a five-year high.

13

Small-cap marvels

I have been an avid follower of the small-cap and micro-cap segment of the stock market over the years and no more so when it comes to my stock recommendations for *Investors Chronicle*.

This is partly because the smaller end of the market is more likely to be under-researched by analysts and below the radar of fund managers; and so offers greater potential to uncover undervalued companies trading on anomalous valuations. It's only sensible to target the parts of the market where you expect the best returns to be made. History books reveal some telling statistics too, because over the long run small-caps have produced the greatest investment returns by far, compared with any other segment of the market.

Long-term outperformance

According to the Numis Smaller Companies Index (NSCI), which covers the bottom tenth of the UK stock market by market value, the small-cap segment has produced a compound annual return of 15.5 per cent since 1955, compared with 11.9 per cent on the FTSE All-Share index. And it's not as though this is a small sample of companies, there were no fewer than 751 companies in the NSCI at the start of 2013.

It was more of the same in 2012, with the NSCI, excluding investment companies, soaring almost 30 per cent and beating the 12.3 per cent return on the FTSE All-Share index handsomely. It's not just a UK phenomenon either. London Business School emeritus professors Elroy Dimson and Paul Marsh, who undertake the research for investment bank Numis, note some interesting findings if the data is widened to incorporate international markets.

In fact, smaller companies in 26 of the 30 global markets monitored by the authors, outperformed larger companies by an average of 5 per cent a year between 2000 and 2012. With an excess average return of that magnitude for small, over large-cap companies, it clearly pays financial rewards to focus on the smaller end of the market.

Dividends pay

It makes sense to focus on the best dividend-paying companies within the small-cap segment. That's because Professors Dimson and Marsh found that, since 1955, the highest yielding small-caps have produced an average annualised total return of 18.4 per cent, whereas the lowest yielders have returned 13.6 per cent a year on average. Non-dividend payers have performed relatively badly, having returned a 9.1 per cent annualised total return over the same 56-year period. High yield and low yield is defined as the 30 per cent highest and lowest yielding stocks at the start of each year in the NSCI.

The trend for the highest yielding small-caps to outperform the lowest yielders was seen once again in 2012, when there was an 8 percentage point difference in the annual total return between the two segments in favour of high yielders.

Value pays too

It's not just high-yielding small-cap stocks that produce above-average returns. Value stocks do too. By ranking small-cap stocks in the NSCI by their ratio of equity book value to market value, there is a clear bias for value to outperform growth. In fact, by defining the 40 per cent highest book-to-market group as value stocks, and the 40 per cent lowest book-to-market group as growth stocks, since 1955 value has outperformed growth by 3 per cent a year. Value stocks have also beaten growth over the past 10 and 20 years.

However, it is worth noting that this is not a one-way bet. Between 2007 and 2011, the growth category of small-cap stocks handsomely outperformed value. Still, small-cap value stocks returned to favour in 2012, outperforming growth by 13 per cent in the 12-month period based on the above selection criteria.

Momentum's a small-cap winner

You can also make money from momentum strategies in the small-cap arena. In the 2012 NSCI Annual Review, Numis revealed that a strategy of buying prior year winners outperformed prior year losers by an eye-catching 21 per cent (before dealing costs) in 2012.

This involves ranking stocks by their returns over the past 12 months. The winners are defined as the top 20 per cent of performers and losers as the bottom 20 per cent. To calculate the subsequent returns from each category, Numis waited one month before investing for one month in the winners and losers. The process is then repeated each month, by rebalancing the holdings in both categories as some companies drop out from their position as winners and losers based on their previous 12-monthly return.

And 2012 was not a one-off. Based on data going all the way back to 1955, winners have outperformed losers by a margin of 17 per cent a year.

Lower volatility boosts returns

In the 2012 NSCI Annual Review, Numis also noted that, over the past 34 years, small-cap stocks with higher levels of company-specific risk have underperformed. In fact, Professors Dimson and Marsh found that, since 1978, low-volatility small-cap shares have produced an annualised return 5.4 per cent above that on high-volatility shares.

Key lessons to learn:

- **Small-cap income stocks.** Focus on the highest yielders to generate the highest returns over the long run.

■ **Price-to-book value.** Value stocks win hands down here over the long run, but there are risks. That's because value stocks have historically performed badly in recessions. This explains why UK small-cap growth stocks outperformed value – based on their ratio of equity book value to market value – between 2007 and 2011, a period characterised by two recessions in the UK and anaemic growth rates in GDP outside recession.

■ **Momentum.** The lesson here is clear: focus on the top small-cap winners until the momentum starts to wane. When this happens, this is the cue to replace the former momentum winners with the new winners based on their previous 12-month share price performance.

■ **Volatility.** Lower volatility small-cap shares not only make it easier to sleep at night, but they produce better long-term returns than more volatile small-cap shares.

14

Contrarian investing

In the previous chapter I highlighted how to enhance portfolio performance by targeting small-cap companies trading on low price-to-book value ratios, and paying above-average dividend yields.

It is possible to take this one stage further by introducing additional selection criteria to narrow down the shortlist of potential investments. One way is to focus on contrarian investment strategies. Perhaps one of the best-known proponents of contrarian investing is David Dreman, the founder, chairman and chief investment officer of US fund management group Dreman Value Management.

Mr Dreman sums up his style as follows: "I buy stocks when they are really battered. I am very strict with my discipline." The top fund manager also adds behavioural finance to his selection process, noting that: "Psychology is probably the most important factor in the market, and the one least understood. There's constant overreaction in the market. Low PE ratio stocks are constantly priced too cheaply over long periods of time, and higher PE ratio stocks are priced too dearly." (*Investors Chronicle*, 'How to screen for contrarian shares', 26 August 2005).

Mr Dreman's focus is firmly on the large-cap segment of the stock market, as these companies are deemed less risky. That's a fair comment to a certain degree; but equally, if you can identify companies fitting his criteria in the small-cap arena, then given the historic outperformance of small-caps over large-caps, as highlighted in previous chapters, this offers potential for even greater returns by following his investment strategy.

Strict criteria to uncover value

Mr Dreman avoids highly indebted companies, and ones of a speculative nature with little, or no track record of earnings. In fact, the key is to identify companies with a decent track record of earnings that are currently being undervalued, but will in time offer potential to enjoy a higher rating. Mr Dreman screens for companies exhibiting the following criteria:

■ Strong fundamentals.

■ High dividend yield.

■ Historic earnings growth.

■ Sustainable earnings growth in future.

■ Low price-to-book value (PTBV).

■ Low price-to-cash flow (PCF).

■ Decent dividend cover, so payout is secure.

■ Strong liquidity ratios.

■ Excellent debt management.

■ Healthy return on equity.

Earnings expectations

Importantly there's one further selection criteria for a Dreman stock screen, and one that I have incorporated into a significant number of my share recommendations for *Investors Chronicle* over the years:

■ Target companies with potential for positive earnings surprises.

In Mr Dreman's studies of earnings surprises, he found that US shares with low PE ratios reacted more strongly to positive earnings surprises than did high PE ratio stocks. That's because positive earnings surprises for out-of-favour stocks are viewed by the market as significant events. Mr Dreman terms them "event triggers" because they initiate a perceptual change among investors.

Therefore, by buying shares that are fundamentally undervalued and that have a realistic prospect of surprising investors to the upside, this provides the necessary catalyst for out-of-favour shares to be rerated.

Long-term rewards

Mr Dreman noted that the returns made by buying solid companies that are currently out of favour, as measured by their low PE, PCF or PTBV ratios, or by their high yields, has stood the test of time. "Over almost every period measured, the stocks considered to have the best prospects fared significantly worse than the contrarian stocks."

This also highlights the important point that investors have a habit of overvaluing companies with the best earnings visibility. And by chasing prices up so high, this means future returns are far more likely to disappoint. It also persuaded me to adopt Dreman's stock selection process as part of my stock screening in the small-cap arena.

Simon Thompson's modified Dreman small-cap stock screen

The criteria I use are as follows:

- Market value below £150m.

- Low PE ratio, or low PTBV, or low PCF.

- Improved EPS growth in the most recent six-month period.

- Above-average forecast EPS growth.

- Return on equity above 10 per cent, a measure of underlying business quality.

- Gearing of less than 75 per cent.

- A current ratio of at least 1. This is a measure of easily realisable assets and indicates a business that can cope with the unexpected.

- Above-average five-year compound average dividend growth.

- A payout ratio (the amount of net profits paid to shareholders as dividends) of two-thirds or under. This means the company is not overstretching itself with the current level of dividend.

To demonstrate how I have used this particular stock screen to uncover small-cap stocks with potential to generate substantial future returns, consider the following case study.

case study 27

Positive earnings and dividend momentum

Imagine being able to buy an income share offering a yield of well over 5 per cent, and with prospects of the company growing earnings and dividends in double-digit rates in the years to come. And don't for one moment think that the current dividend is not well covered by net earnings. In fact, it was covered a healthy 1.5 times in 2012 and will be in the future too. That's because the board has pledged to pay out two-thirds of net earnings as dividends.

This was the attractive prospect offered by Aim-traded Jarvis Securities, a stockbroker and financial services outsource provider, when I highlighted the investment case (*Investors Chronicle*, 'Solid income buy', 25 February 2013). The company was founded in 1984 and has been led by chief executive and chairman Andrew Grant ever since. Jarvis is a member of the London Stock Exchange and was first quoted on the Alternative Investment Market in 2004.

The Dreman screen
Applying my Dreman-derived stock screen, Jarvis immediately ticked five of my criteria: high dividend yield; good dividend cover; rising dividend; prospect of earnings growth; and market value

below £150m. The shares were modestly rated too, priced on 13 times historic earnings, following a 20 per cent rise in net profits in 2012. There was also positive earnings momentum in the business. In fact, reflecting a growing suite of products being marketed to a wider and larger client base, management was "confident of continuing the double-digit growth".

Analysts had lifted earnings forecasts following the company's full-year results, but not by too much for another upgrade to be out of the question as the financial year progressed. Furthermore, given the stated payout ratio, the earnings upgrades secured a further rise in the dividend in 2013 to maintain the progressive dividend policy.

Jarvis was also in a cash-rich position, so there were no financial worries: the net cash pile had trebled in 2012, and equated to 15 per cent of the company's market value of £23m; and the current ratio (of current assets over current liabilities) was comfortable at 1.25.

Solid income streams

The company's business model was attractive. In terms of income generation, around £2.8m of revenues in 2012 came from interest earned on broking accounts, cash in the bank and overdrawn client accounts; with the balance of £3.3m earned mainly from fees and commissions. Cash under administration had averaged around £70m for the past couple of years and is normally placed on a short-term deposit of less than one year, with triple-A-rated banks. That was worth noting, because when interest rates start to return to more normal levels, the hike in interest income will provide significant profit upside to Jarvis.

Even in a low-interest-rate environment Jarvis was still hugely profitable. EPS was forecast to rise a further 9 per cent in 2013, which would underpin a further rise in the dividend. Return on equity was eye-catching: post-tax profits equated to 70 per cent of shareholder funds, and growing.

Ticking all the boxes

Jarvis hit all nine of my Dreman-derived selection criteria. Importantly, with earnings more likely to surprise to the upside, there was also a possible catalyst for a rerating in the coming months. For good measure, a share price that had traded sideways for 18 months was nearing the top of its trading range, so offering the possibility of a chart break-out. An upbeat trading update at the annual meeting did just that and Jarvis's shares subsequently soared 26 per cent from my recommended buy-in price within six weeks.

15

Bargain shares

B enjamin Graham, the father of value investing, once said: "If we assume that it is the habit of the market to overvalue common stocks which have been showing excellent growth, or are glamorous for some other reason, it is logical to expect that it will undervalue – relatively at least – companies that are out of favour because of unsatisfactory developments of a temporary nature. This may be set down as a fundamental law of the stock market, and it suggests an investment approach that should be both conservative and promising." That, in a nutshell, is what my annual bargain shares portfolios in *Investors Chronicle* are all about.

The idea behind bargain shares is very simple. It's to invest in companies where the true worth of the assets is not reflected in the share price, usually for some temporary reason, but where we can reasonably expect that it will become apparent in due course.

Impressive track record

It is the very essence of stock picking, and whatever fans of passive investment might say, it works: £10,000 invested a decade ago in my *Investors Chronicle* bargain shares portfolio in February 2003, and reinvested every subsequent year in the following annual bargain shares portfolio, would have grown by almost 400 per cent in value to £49,600 by early February 2013. To put this performance into perspective, the same investment in a FTSE All-Share index tracker would be worth under £26,000 including the reinvestment of dividends.

| Table 15.1 | Bargain shares portfolio: 10-year track record |

Year	Bargain portfolio 1-year performance (%)
2003	146.0
2004	17.1
2005	50.0
2006	16.9
2007	-0.9
2008	-60.1
2009	53.4
2010	50.4
2011	-18.4
2012	31.9
Compound annual return	**17.3**
FTSE All-Share (including reinvestment of dividends)	10.0
Annual outperformance	**7.3**

Source: *Investors Chronicle*, 'Bargain shares 2013', 8 February 2013

And my 2012 motley crew of bargain shares (*Investors Chronicle*, 'Bargain shares 2012', 10 February 2012) maintained this impressive track record, producing a total return of 31.9 per cent on an offer-to-bid basis. This was largely down to the fact that my portfolio was entirely small-cap based – a segment of the market that has benefited greatly from the marked improvement in investor sentiment since the summer of 2012. This performance compares very favourably with the 13.4 per cent total return on the FTSE All-Share index and the 22.7 per cent total return on the FTSE SmallCap index in the same 12-month period (after factoring in dividend income).

My 2012 bargain shares portfolio only marginally lagged behind the total return of 34.6 per cent on the Fidelity UK Smaller Caps Fund, the best-performing small-cap fund out of the 56 funds in this segment in the same period, according to Trustnet. This was no fluke, because over the long run my record of stock picking by using this investment technique has stood the test of time, and is in no small part down to the stellar performance from the undervalued small-cap shares I have consistently uncovered.

Table 15.2   Bargain shares 2012 portfolio performance

Company	Share price on 10 February 2012 (p)	Share price on 6 February 2013 (p)	Dividends paid (p)	Total return (%)
Telford Homes	91.7	202	3.5	124.1
MJ Gleeson	110	187	0	70.0
Stanley Gibbons	178	283	6.25	62.5
Molins	107	159	5.25	53.5
Indigovision	325	316	80	21.8
Trading Emissions	25.25	23	6	14.9
Bloomsbury Publishing	115	114	5.25	3.7
Mallett	73	67	0	-8.2
Rugby Estates	433	330	250	-9.6
Eurovestech	9.3	6.75	1.32	-13.2
Average				**31.9**
FTSE All-Share	3044	3315		13.4
FTSE SmallCap	3051	3642		22.7

Source: *Investors Chronicle*, 'Bargain shares 2012 update', 8 February 2013

Bumper gains

My 2003 bargain shares portfolio for example, rocketed by 146 per cent in its first 12 months, and if you held onto the shares, the portfolio then increased in value by a further 50 per cent in the following two years, to produce a three-year return of 270 per cent. My 2004 portfolio produced a 17.1 per cent return in its first 12 months and then rose in value by a further 36 per cent in its second year to produce a 24-month return of 59.6 per cent.

True, the collapse in share prices following the stock market crash in 2008 wreaked havoc with that year's portfolio, but *Investors Chronicle* readers who kept faith subsequently recovered all their paper losses, which highlights the solid asset backing of the companies recommended. In fact, two of those companies from the 2008 bargain shares portfolio – Bollywood film producer Indian Film Company and property company Raven Mount – succumbed to takeovers.

Merger and acquisition (M&A) activity has been a recurring feature of all my portfolios. Two companies from my 2009 portfolio – vehicle tracking company Trafficmaster and investment company GNE – were both taken over. It was a similar story in 2010, when general industrial manufacturer Delta was bid for within a couple of months of making it into my portfolio. These gains helped both the 2009 and 2010 portfolios to soar in value, producing 12-monthly gains of 53 per cent and 50 per cent respectively, including dividend income. So how do I manage to achieve these impressive returns?

Table 15.3   Bargain shares 2009 portfolio performance

Company	Share price on 6 February 2009 (p)	Share price on 1 February 2010 (p)	Dividends paid (p)	Total return (%)
BATM Communciations	24	54.25	0	126.0
Trafficmaster	16	33	0	106.3
Trikona Trinity Capital	34	47	0	38.2
Mallett	50	71	0	42.0
GNE	150	190	0	26.7
French Connection	48	39	0	-18.8
Average return				**53.4**
FTSE All-Share	2118	2661		29.7

Source: *Investors Chronicle*, 'Bargain shares 2009 update', 12 February 2010

| Table 15.4 | Bargain shares 2010 portfolio performance |

Company	Share price on 11 February 2010 (p)	Share price on 8 February 2011 (p)	Dividends paid (p)	Total return (%)
Bowleven	113.5	294	0	159.0
Acal	141	336	7.0	143.3
KBC Advanced Technologies	45	70	5.64	68.1
Delta	140	185	4.8	35.6
Jacques Vert	16.25	16.75	0.65	7.1
Gleeson (MJ)	130	118.25	15.0	2.5
Bloomsbury Publishing	124	114.25	4.4	-4.3
Telford Homes	91	81	2.5	-8.2
Average				**50.4**
FTSE All-Share	2,644	3,135		23.1

Source: *Investors Chronicle*, 'Bargain shares', 8 February 2011

Investment technique

My annual bargain shares portfolios are based on the writings of Benjamin Graham, a US investor and writer. The author of the seminal 1949 work *The Intelligent Investor*, he is considered to be the father of value investing.

Mr Graham's approach was to focus on the balance sheet of a company, and specifically the net current assets – stocks, debtors and cash less any creditors. He believed that a bargain share is one where net current assets, less all prior obligations, exceed the market value of the company by at least 50 per cent. Mr Graham's theory was that a strong balance sheet will usually see a company through any short-term difficulties; he called it his "margin of safety".

Finding companies that match these strict criteria has become more and more difficult over the years, as the link between market capitalisation and asset value has become more tenuous. In practice, only a handful of the 1,750 listed UK companies on the London Stock Exchange and Alternative Investment Market (Aim) have a bargain ratio of 1 or above.

Furthermore, the ones that do include a large number of illiquid small companies with market values well below £10m. These are very difficult to trade. So to widen the net, I use a cut-off point of around 0.4 for my bargain ratio.

Calculating a bargain ratio

To illustrate how this works, consider a company with a market value of £100m, net asset value of £140m, fixed assets of £40m and net current assets less all liabilities of £100m. So the ratio between net current assets less all liabilities (£100m) and market value (£100m) is 1. This means all the fixed assets of £40m are in the price for free. It's really that simple. It's also an incredibly reliable way of uncovering shares with potential to generate significant gains over the long term.

It's worth noting that the number of companies with a bargain ratio of at least 1 rises markedly at the end of bear markets. That's because shares become heavily oversold and valuations fall well below fair value due to the extreme levels of negative investor sentiment and high risk aversion. This explains why my bargain shares portfolios in both 2003 and 2009, which were published within a few weeks of the end of respective equity bear markets, produced such spectacular returns. There were rich pickings indeed as I will explain in my case studies later.

Top 10 rules for screening bargain shares

■ **Invest for the medium term**. Although my annual bargain shares portfolios for *Investors Chronicle* have performed very well over the years, and some portfolios have racked up sharp gains in a short time frame, you should always remember that value investing is for the patient. As was the case in 2008, you may find yourself in for a couple of years with some companies before reaping the rewards.

This was also true of my 2011 portfolio. Heightened investor risk aversion, as the eurozone sovereign debt crisis worsened, meant the small-cap segment of the market was largely shunned by investors that year. However, the paper losses made in the 2011 portfolio have narrowed substantially since, as in more benign equity market conditions, investors focus on the investment merits of the companies.

▪ **Diversify risk**. It is important to buy a decent number of shares matching the bargain shares criteria to diversify risk. Otherwise you could be unfortunate enough to select the only loser from your shortlist of companies.

▪ **Liquidity**. Avoid companies where the bid-offer spread is above 4 per cent, otherwise you are creating a massive hurdle for yourself in trying to outperform the market. Remember, my bargain shares portfolios have on average produced an annual investment return 7 percentage points more than the FTSE All-Share index in the past decade. This has been achieved by focusing on companies that are relatively easy to trade and where the bid-offer spread is not eating up a chunk of capital to start with.

▪ **Time your entry point**. Don't feel you have to jump in as soon as you uncover a bargain share. As I have outlined in previous chapters, shares in companies in different sectors perform well at certain times of the year, and badly at others, mainly due to seasonal investing patterns. Therefore, it's best to do your research and create a watchlist of bargain shares first. Then time your entry point to maximise returns by buying when the shares are likely to be most undervalued, or alternatively at the point when seasonal investing patterns are turning in your favour.

▪ **Pick stocks wisely**. Some companies have high bargain ratios because they are incredibly risky. You should never buy blind – this is a recipe for disaster. Do your fundamental research and then decide whether the investment case is sound, and whether the potential share price upside is large enough to warrant investing. I research the investment case of over 100 companies in January each year before whittling my shortlist down to a bargain shares portfolio of no more than 10 shares.

▪ **Investment companies.** A number of my bargain share selections over the years have been investment companies that have been trading at huge discounts to net asset value, even though there is a plan in place to return cash to shareholders. The return of cash can create a strong share price tailwind for a rerating once a wider investor audience becomes aware of it.

▪ **Avoid highly geared companies.** It is best to avoid companies carrying very high levels of balance sheet gearing, for the simple fact that some bargain shares carry higher operational risk due to a temporary period of adverse trading. It's fine taking on operational risk when the low valuation offers adequate compensation, but potential gains would have to be significant if you are taking on large amounts of financial risk at the same time. Sometimes the risk can be too great to warrant an investment.

■ **Set price targets.** To quantify the potential upside and downside risk, it's best to estimate a best-case scenario and a worst-case scenario for each bargain share. This way you can weigh up the potential upside for a portfolio of these bargain shares, while knowing the amount of risk you are taking on in your shareholdings. Personally, I attempt to create a portfolio where the upside potential is double the downside risk.

■ **Set price limits**. It's well worth setting a price at which you believe the potential future returns from an investment warrant buying shares in a company. This not only introduces discipline into the share buying process, but also means that you can create a watchlist of companies that may not necessarily warrant an investment at the current price, but could prove an attractive investment opportunity to exploit in the event of a short-term price correction.

■ **Understand bargain ratios**. A company with a high bargain ratio will not necessarily produce the greatest future returns. This investment technique uncovers medium-term shareholdings with potential to outperform the benchmark FTSE All-Share index, but there are various factors that determine the degree of the outperformance.

For instance, consider the case of a cash-rich investment company in the process of winding itself up. All the assets are up for sale and are deemed current assets in the accounts, so the company has no fixed assets. Let's also assume that the market value of the company is 20 per cent below its net asset value. On this basis, the bargain ratio is 1.25 because net current assets less all liabilities exceed the market value by 25 per cent. It also means that the maximum upside is no more than 25 per cent, as the maximum amount that can be paid back to shareholders is the net asset value of the company, assuming disposals of assets are booked at their carrying value.

Let's also assume that another company has a bargain rating of 1.25. However this company is a cash-rich industrial business enjoying improving cash flow generation and a recovery in profits. As momentum gathers in the recovery, the scope for this company's shares to re-rate is significantly more than the aforementioned investment company, because the share price can easily move from a discount to book value to a sizeable premium.

To highlight how I go about uncovering bargain shares each year using the above investment techniques, consider the following four case studies.

case study 28

Capitalising on cash-rich companies

Imagine being able to buy £1 of assets for just 57p. Even better, imagine all of the £1 of assets is in cash. It may seem incredible, but this was the investment opportunity on offer in early 2009 when I included shares in GNE in my bargain shares portfolio (*Investors Chronicle*, 'Bargain shares portfolio 2009', 6 February 2009).

At the time, the investment company had just sold off its main petrol station operations in a £51.6m cash transaction. That allowed GNE to pay down all its borrowings. Apart from some remaining commercial property assets and a very small fuel cards business, the company was sitting on £36.7m of net cash, worth 263p a share, in line with its net asset value at the end of 2008.

Despite this chunky cash pile, shares in GNE were trading at only 150p, valuing the company at just £20.9m. In other words, a not inconsiderable 113p-a-share of cash was in the price for free. So strip out fixed assets of £2.2m from the net asset value, and GNE had net current assets less all liabilities of £34.5m. This was 1.7 times its market value of £20.9m, so the bargain rating was 1.7.

The company had been intending to return 150p-a-share cash to shareholders through a special dividend, but those plans changed when a concert party controlling 28.7 per cent of the share capital approached the board. Led by Martyn Ratcliffe, chairman of small-cap software company Microgen, the party proposed to turn GNE into an investment trust focused on the technology sector.

True, it was possible that if shareholders approved the change in strategic direction the new management team could destroy value by making some poor investments. However, it was worth noting that Mr Ratcliffe had bought a 15 per cent stake in GNE and had been appointed to the board, so he had a clear vested interest in enhancing shareholder returns. He also had the backing of North Atlantic Smaller Companies Trust, which controlled just under 12 per cent of GNE's share capital.

Something had to give – and it did. Five weeks after my 2009 bargain shares portfolio was published in the *Investors Chronicle*, GNE received a cash bid at 190p a share, valuing the company at £26.4m. Mr Ratcliffe and North Atlantic Smaller Companies had teamed up to take the company private, and with backing from shareholders accounting for a further 27 per cent of GNE's issued share capital, it was a done deal. True, the 190p-a-share cash bid was well below the level of the company's cash pile, but it also delivered a 26 per cent share price gain in only five weeks.

Key lessons to learn:

■ Cash-rich companies mitigate investment risk, especially if there is potential for some of the cash to be returned to shareholders.

■ GNE had already disposed of its main assets so investment risk was further reduced.

■ Two major shareholders controlled almost 27 per cent of GNE's issued share capital and one of them, North Atlantic Smaller Companies Trust, was a shareholder activist. This meant there was potential for some corporate activity.

■ Even if GNE had become a technology-focused investment company, the share price was already trading 43 per cent below end-December 2008 book value. This meant the risk associated with the proposed change of direction was more than factored into the share price in early 2009.

case study 29

Legislative changes drive share prices

Molins is a specialist engineering business, and one that was well below the radar of most investors when I selected it as one of my bargain shares of 2012 (*Investors Chronicle*, 'Bargain shares for 2012', 10 February 2012). That's because the Milton Keynes-based company had a market value of £21.2m at the time, so would not have been of interest to the majority of fund managers.

As a result the company's share price had yet to factor in news that profits were on an upward trajectory, and with margins on a number of projects expected to show improvement, the underlying performance had strengthened further.

Understand the business

Two-thirds of the company's sales come from the tobacco industry, including the manufacture and servicing of tobacco processing machinery. Molins also specialises in improving the effectiveness of existing customer plant, monitoring and testing product quality and conducting the analysis of cigarette smoke. This is the high-end part of the business.

By its nature, the business carries a variety of risks; none more so than macro risk as a changing economic climate impacts upon order visibility and can lead to cancellations. Molins also carries currency risk; less than 15 per cent of sales are in the UK, and manufacturing facilities are located in a number of countries overseas. There is competition in the aftermarket from third-party suppliers too.

Attractive fundamentals

Still, risk warnings aside, there was a lot to like about the company in early February 2012.

■ Molins was valued on less than half book value even though it had net cash of £6.3m – the equivalent of 31p a share, or 30 per cent of the 107p share price.

■ Modest growth in underlying operating profits forecast, so cash pile set to rise further.

■ Dividend of 5p-a-share almost three times covered by underlying EPS of 14p to offer an attractive yield of 5 per cent.

■ Low PE ratio of 7.

■ Net asset value of £41m included fixed assets of £29.9m. This meant Molins had net current assets less all liabilities of £11.1m, which compared favourably with a market value of £21m to give a bargain share ratio of 0.5.

It's one thing to have an attractive investment case, but what investors contemplating buying shares in Molins really needed was a potential catalyst for a share price rerating. That was firmly on the cards over the coming year, as the US regulator the Federal Drugs Administration (FDA), was expected to introduce legislation to tighten up the testing requirements for tobacco companies in the country.

Share price rerating driven by new regulation

By having an onshore US testing facility, Molins had a significant logistical and marketing advantage to attract business for its testing services. That was important, because the new FDA consultation list had over 90 harmful compounds that could be tested (correct as of October 2012), compared with only 20 that were subject to previous testing. As a result, industry analysts believed that several of the major tobacco manufacturers, who currently do the testing of these compounds in-house, would outsource much of it in future if the FDA tightened up the testing regime; this could offer a real opportunity for Molins to grow its testing business.

In my view, it was the combination of positive newsflow from the company on the trading front, and the prospect for growth in its US testing business, that sent shares in the company soaring. In fact, within a year Molins' share price had risen 50 per cent and shareholders had also banked a raised dividend of 5.25p a share.

Key lessons to learn:

■ Molins was undervalued on any basis in February 2012, but a catalyst was needed to spark a share price rerating. By investigating potential growth areas of the business, I discovered that legislation changes in the US could be of major significance for Molins and support a rerating.

■ Earnings expectations were modest, so risk to earnings was weighted to the upside.

■ Scope for a higher payout, reflecting a burgeoning cash pile. In fact, the board raised the dividend from 5p a share in 2010, to 5.25p a share in 2011 and 5.5p a share in 2012.

■ Hefty cash pile mitigated investment risk.

case study 30

Blue-sky profits

When Kevin Hart, chief executive of BowLeven reported his group's preliminary results in November 2009, he noted that "2010 is shaping up to be the most active period in the West African oil and gas exploration group's history.... with a scheduled work programme that will shape its history." A drilling campaign in the shallow waters of the Etinde Permit off the coast of Cameroon would determine whether this optimism was well placed.

The omens looked good when I included BowLeven in my 2010 bargain shares portfolio (*Investors Chronicle*, 'Bargain shares for 2010', 12 February 2010). The company had already drilled four wells on the permit in the previous three years, and all had been successful. Moreover, Swiss oil investment company Vitol was certainly bullish, having agreed to fund a $100m (£61.5m) gross work programme in return for a 25 per cent interest in Etinde. It had an option to acquire a further 25 per cent interest in the project in return for funding an additional $100m gross work programme, as well as paying BowLeven $25m in cash.

Drilling activity accelerated

The plan was to drill four further wells on Etinde with the aim of proving up reserves and commercialising the discoveries towards production. The first work was scheduled for April/May 2010, with the spudding of an appraisal well on the important Isongo E field, which brokers thought could hold 32m barrels of recoverable gas condensate, and 27m barrels of oil equivalent of gas. The company would then drill an appraisal well on the Isongo F field, which could feasibly hold between 53m and 80m barrels of oil, before focusing on high-impact exploration activity.

Activity in Cameroon aside, BowLeven planned to drill an exploration well on the Epaemeno Permit, offshore Gabon, in which the company had a 50 per cent non-operated equity interest alongside partner Addax Petroleum.

Compelling investment

What made BowLeven a compelling investment at the time was that all this drilling activity was largely in the price for free. That's because:

■ BowLeven had net assets of $426m, which equated to £263m, or 136p a share. That was 20 per cent more than its market value of £218m with the shares priced at only 113p in February 2010.

■ Some of the assets were effectively being attributed no value at all, and that's before factoring in a potential fillip from a successful drilling campaign.

■ With Vitol on board to fund a large part of the works, and BowLeven sitting on $110m of net cash at the end of December 2009, the company was in a very strong financial position.

True, the shares had a higher risk profile due to the nature and location of the business, but on a deep discount to book value and rated on a bargain rating of 0.42, they offered scope for the discount to narrow markedly if the exploration campaign went well. In fact, it paid dirt big time.

By November 2010, BowLeven's share price had soared 159 per cent in value following upbeat exploration news, including two "potentially significant" discoveries at its Sapele-1 well on block MLHP-5 on the Etinde permit. I conservatively advised that readers of *Investors Chronicle* should consider banking profits at this time, having seen the share price rise from 113.5p in February to 294p. Two months later the price hit an all-time high of 414p, a gain of 264 per cent in only 11 months after my recommendation to buy in February 2010.

Key lessons to learn:

■ Exploration companies are risky by their nature, but if they are being priced substantially below book value, and drilling activities are already funded, this mitigates risk.

■ BowLeven was in a strong financial position so was under no pressure to raise fresh funds to finance the drilling campaign. In fact, the farm-out agreement with Vitol had passed much of the risk on to another party.

■ BowLeven had a proven track record of successful drilling which reduced the risk of an unsuccessful campaign.

■ Potential resource estimates, if firmed up, were material relative to the £218m market value of BowLeven. Any positive newsflow to confirm major discoveries had the potential to send the share price soaring.

case study 31

Investing in companies winding up

When Aim-traded Trading Emissions started life eight years ago its main investment objective was to make capital profits from purchasing emissions assets in the European economic area. To say that it hasn't been a success for shareholders would not be an understatement.

By the start of 2012, investors who had backed the float in April 2005, when the company raised £135m, and those that participated in a £175m secondary placing 12 months later, had seen the value of their investments plunge by 75 per cent in value.

At a bombed-out 25.25p, the company was worth just £67m, having steadily fallen from above the 100p-a-share float price in the previous eight months. Plans to sell off both the private equity portfolio and carbon portfolio in their entirety had bombed too, and the company was now selling off investments on an individual basis, with the intention of returning cash to shareholders.

Bargain basement rating

So with investor sentiment dire, the shares were being priced on a vast discount to net asset value of 76.7p a share. The carbon portfolio was worthless – it had a negative worth of 6.4p a share – and the company's unhedged exposure to carbon obligations for pre-December 2012 delivery had a maximum liability, the equivalent of 31p a share. True, that was in the unlikely event that the carbon price fell to zero, but if it happened, Trading Emissions' net asset value would plunge further to 46.7p a share.

Still, I could see value in the company and included the shares, at 25.25p, in my 2012 bargain shares portfolio (*Investors Chronicle*, 'Bargain shares for 2012', 10 February 2012). That's because Trading Emissions had the money to honour these carbon obligations as the company held cash of £65m at the time – so the shares were trading in line with net cash. But this failed to take into account a private equity portfolio worth 60p a share.

True, these are illiquid investments and a discount should be applied to value the portfolio on a fire-sale basis. But even factoring in a hefty 50 per cent write-off on these private equity investments, a further £10m in wind-up costs for the company and a carbon price of nil value, Trading Emissions still had a break-up value around 28p a share, well above the company's share price in February 2012. This extreme valuation left the risk to the share price firmly to the upside if Trading Emissions announced any positive newsflow. And that is precisely what happened in the subsequent 12 months.

Catalyst for rerating

The catalyst for the subsequent share price rerating was threefold.

▪ **Improved disclosure**. In subsequent results releases Trading Emissions' management went into great detail about how it was containing the carbon liabilities. In turn, this enabled investors to get a grip on what the underlying value in the business really was, and importantly, how much of the net assets were likely to be returned to shareholders as Trading Emissions wound itself up.

▪ **Large disposals made**. Importantly, these asset sales were made close to their carrying value, which highlighted the anomalous share price discount to the company's net asset value.

▪ **Capital return**. Trading Emissions not only returned 6p a share to investors in January 2013, but a few months later announced that a further distribution to shareholders was "expected to be announced in the second quarter this year".

By late April 2013, shares in Trading Emissions had risen to 29p, and this was after the payment of the 6p-a-share dividend in January 2013. Adjust for that payout and investors following my advice to buy in February 2012 were now holding shares worth 29p for a net investment of only 19.25p, and with the prospect of more substantial capital returns to come.

Key lessons to learn:

▪ **Look for share price catalysts.** In the case of Trading Emissions it was improved disclosure by the board, disposals made, and imminent capital returns that focused investor attention and sparked the rerating.

▪ **Take the worst-case scenario.** If a company is under no financial pressure to make disposals, but is being priced below break-up value, any positive news on asset sales will force investors to reassess the investment case.

▪ **Understand the cash position.** Trading Emissions was able to hold out for the best prices on its disposals because the company was a willing seller, not a forced seller. This fact alters the investment case materially. That's because the shares were being priced at a level that implied the company was in financial distress in the first quarter of 2012 – when it clearly wasn't.

At that time, the shares were trading 10 per cent below the worst-case scenario break-up value, and one that factored in a 50 per cent haircut to the private equity portfolio and a carbon price of nil value. Investors may have acknowledged the size of the net cash position, but not the importance of it in allowing the company to have the time to make disposals at levels materially in excess of fire-sale values.

16

Portfolio management

When the greatest investor of all time, Warren Buffett, was asked to describe himself, he said: "85 per cent Graham and 15 per cent Fisher." That's quite some accolade to Benjamin Graham, the father of value investing, on whose works I have based my annual bargain shares portfolios. It also speaks volumes of the influence that Philip Fisher, a highly respected American investor and the founder of investment management company Fisher & Co, has on the investment approach of Mr Buffett.

Not only did Mr Fisher have a brilliant talent, but he talked a lot of sense, and no more so when asked to single out the most important lesson he had learned from his career as an investor. The response is worth repeating: "It is just appalling the nerve strain people put themselves under trying to buy something today and sell it tomorrow. It's a small-win proposition. If you are a truly long-range investor, of which I am practically a vanishing breed, the profits are so tremendously greater."

That rings a chord with my own investment style, which is to run my profits on a shareholding until it becomes obvious that the rationale for making the investment in the first place no longer holds. It also rings true with the timescale I am working to for the majority of my value-focused share recommendations.

Namely, if the rationale behind the decision to invest is sound, and the investment case doesn't diminish during the holding period, then it is only realistic to expect valuation anomalies to be arbitraged away as soon as enough other like-minded value investors discover them. This process could take weeks or even months, but ultimately the odds favour a positive outcome in time.

So to maximise the chances of making the greatest returns by taking the least amount of risk, I set some guidelines in my portfolio management to avoid the pitfalls of generating less than favourable returns for the risk taken.

Guidelines for successful portfolio management

■ **Focus on shares with potential to generate significant returns over the medium to long term.** If these gains are made sooner, that's a bonus, but never count on it. Remember, investing is a marathon and not a sprint.

■ **Set a realistic time frame for gains to be achieved.** If an investment is only likely to produce a modest return, then it's only worth investing if the time horizon is short and the risk is low. Otherwise, the annualised return on your capital diminishes rapidly the longer you have to wait for an investment to come good.

■ **Be patient.** Even if a potential investment ticks all the right boxes, there is one thing worse than not being invested. That's being invested at the wrong price. Timing is everything in investing and it always pays to be patient. Only purchase shares in a company when the future potential return embedded in the share price is satisfactory for the risk being taken.

■ **Don't ignore dividends.** If an investor can make a return of 12 per cent a year on a portfolio, with the benefit of reinvesting dividends, this translates into a total return of 1,600 per cent over a period of 25 years. But if the starting yield on the portfolio is 4 per cent, this means a third of the targeted annual growth rate is in the bag from the start. Moreover, dividends grow over time and can be reinvested to mitigate risk.

This is why many of the companies I highlight are decent dividend payers. It also explains why you are better off investing in higher-yielding shares for the long run than low yielders. In fact, according to the Credit Suisse Global Investment Returns Handbook, in collaboration with the London

Business School, the difference between the annual total returns on the highest yielding shares (10.9 per cent), and lowest yielding shares (7.8 per cent), on the London stock market has been on average 3.1 per cent a year since 1900. That may not sound much of a difference, but with the benefit of compounding, a portfolio of high-yielding shares would be worth more than double that of the low yielders after 25 years; treble the value of the low yielders after 40 years; and four times larger after 50 years.

■ **Quality wins in the end.** Given the choice between selecting a good-quality company rated on a relatively attractive valuation to its historic average, and with an impressive long-term track record, or a lower-quality company priced on a sub-market earnings multiple, I will always opt for the former. That's because investors are more inclined to pay premium ratings for quality companies. In turn this offers potential for their share prices to recover to (and potentially above) their long-term average earnings multiple. So on a risk-adjusted basis the odds of a favourable outcome are far better.

■ **Spread risk.** As discussed in previous chapters, there are a variety of different risks embedded in the valuations of companies. It therefore pays to spread the risk of the holdings in your portfolio. To do this you should consider the level of risk you are taking on in five key areas: market risk; economic risk; liquidity risk; distress risk; and volatility risk. The idea is to minimise the total amount of risk embedded in each shareholding so that on average your portfolio is less volatile, and less exposed to large amounts of risk in any one of these five areas.

■ **Heed the bigger picture.** In the digital age, newsflow is around the clock and around the world. This offers opportunities to exploit investment opportunities in other markets.

For instance, in early 2013, *Investors Chronicle*'s columnist, the Right Honourable John Baron, explained why he believed "the election of Shinzo Abe as Prime Minister in Japan could be a 'game-changer' – and not yet another false dawn." (*Investors Chronicle*, 'Japan: A once-in-a-lifetime opportunity', 7 February 2013). Mr Abe had won a landslide election – a two-thirds majority – advocating an aggressive programme of fiscal stimulus, despite the size of the budget deficit, and almost unlimited monetary easing. Inflation was now the number one objective.

Mr Baron's logic for investing in Japanese equities was quite compelling: if rising inflation ends the 20-year bull market in bonds – and changes the mindset of the traditionally conservative Japanese investors – the money flowing into bonds would need a new home. And that home would be equities. Other investors clearly had the same idea. Buoyed by a huge new round of quantitative easing (money printing) by the Bank of Japan, the Nikkei 225 index had soared by 20 per cent by late April 2013.

Moreover, movements in the Japanese stock market had become far less correlated with those in other major world bourses, reflecting the country-specific drivers of the rally. Therefore, holding Japanese equities had the effect of diversifying market risk in a well-balanced portfolio, as well as providing bumper gains.

■ **Momentum pays.** Momentum strategies can work well in bull markets in enhancing portfolio returns, by focusing on companies whose shares have been performing well compared with the market. With investor sentiment positive, and equity market conditions benign, this increases the potential for the outperformance to continue. Of course the fundamental case for investing must stack up, but by screening out the best share price performers over the previous three months you can create a shortlist of potential investment opportunities to ride the momentum and enhance portfolio returns.

■ **Avoid 'value traps'.** Some companies are lowly valued for a variety of reasons and not just because they carry more risk than other companies. For instance, they may not be run for the benefit of outside shareholders. As a result investors are simply not prepared to value these companies on anything other than sub-market and sub-sector earnings multiples. These apparent 'value traps' reveal themselves when you carry out the 16 different risk assessment tests I outlined in Chapter 11.

■ **Avoid 'bubbles'.** When share prices are being buoyed by speculation, and undertaking sound fundamental investment analysis is nigh on impossible due to the lack of relevant financial history, then it is best to walk away. The number one rule of investing is not to lose your capital. The obvious way of preventing this happening is to avoid investing in bubbles.

Exit strategies

The benefit of setting a pre-determined target price at which you believe shares in a company offer fair value, is that it enables you to reassess the investment case as, and when, the price hits the target. At this point you have to ask yourself whether the original rationale for making the investment still holds; and quantify whether the upside potential from the investment warrants maintaining the holding, given the downside risk.

If it doesn't, it's time to bank profits. But if there is potential for further upside, put a plan in place to exploit this, and preferably one that reduces risk to the profits already made. There are various strategies to do this, but the one I prefer is to sell half or two-thirds of a holding – a process known as top slicing – and maintain a trailing stop-loss on the balance.

Top slicing and trailing stop-losses

A good example of this was my advice to readers of *Investors Chronicle* to buy shares in the UK's eight listed FTSE 250 housebuilders at the start of 2013 with the intention of benefiting from the historic first-quarter rise in the sector by the end of March (*Investors Chronicle*, 'Foundations for a rally', 12 December 2012).

In the event, the sector soared by 21.7 per cent by the last week of March. My advice at the time was to sell two-thirds of the holdings in each company, and maintain a strict 10 per cent trailing stop-loss on the remainder, in order to protect the paper profits (*Investors Chronicle*, 'Full house', 25 March 2013). I also set a new share price target on each holding, which if achieved was the signal to bank the balance of the profits. The time frame for running these profits was until the end of April.

This meant that an investment of £1,000 in each of the eight companies at the start of 2013 was worth £1,217 by the start of the last week of March. Therefore, by selling two-thirds of each holding, an investor was recouping £806 of the initial £1,000 investment, leaving £411 invested in each company. The strict 10 per cent trailing stop-loss meant that only £41 of capital, or 10 per cent of the £411 remaining investment in each holding was at risk. In other words, of the £1,217 investment in each company, only £41 was being risked after profits had been taken on two-thirds of the holding since a tight trailing stop-loss had been placed on the remainder.

This strategy enabled investors to redeploy 80 per cent of the £1,000 original capital in other investments, while at the same time having some skin left in the game to benefit from any further upside in the housebuilders' shares. As it transpired it was worth doing, because shares in all of the eight companies continued to rally and subsequently achieved my raised target prices by the end of April 2013.

Stop-losses

Clearly, not all investments go to plan. This creates a problem because it raises the difficult decision as to when to exit a poorly performing shareholding. To get around this, some investors use pre-set stop-losses at the time of purchase. These will vary depending on the volatility of the shares, but normally a stop-loss can be anything between 15 per cent and 20 per cent of the initial purchase price.

The advantage of adhering to stop-losses, is that as soon as the stop is triggered the holding is sold and you move on. There is no going back. It also protects the investor from the draining psychological trauma of seeing a share trend ever lower, wiping out larger amounts of capital in the process.

The disadvantage of stop-loss systems, is that sometimes a share price can go through a stop-loss and then rebound immediately. For instance, short-term market sell-offs can lead to heightened risk aversion and sharp falls in share prices, but these can correct themselves very quickly. Investors using stop-losses may well exit their investments during the initial sell-off, only to be out of the market as it recovers all the lost ground.

As a consequence, although I use trailing stop-losses to protect gains, I prefer to address each holding in a portfolio on a case-by-case basis. That way I can ascertain whether it is an operational issue; changes in market risk; technical selling or some other factor that has been driving the price lower, and whether the situation is likely to correct itself in a reasonable time frame. If I conclude that it isn't, then it's time to bail out.

17

Quantitative easing

I f you ever doubted the power of the US Federal Reserve (Fed), the past four years have been a textbook case of how the world's leading central bank continues to have a massive influence on financial markets. And this is all down to a monetary policy known as 'quantitative easing' (QE), otherwise referred to as printing money.

Implications of QE on asset prices

To give you some idea of the positive impact of QE on equities, consider the US central bank's second round of quantitative easing (QE2). This involved a $600bn programme of asset purchases carried out between October 2010 and June 2011.

The permanent open market operations (POMO) of the New York Federal Reserve proved not only supportive of the short-dated end of the US Treasury bond market, whereby the US central bank bought in government bonds on specific dates as part of a short-term asset purchase programme, but liquidity was clearly flowing out of US government bonds into equity markets. In fact, in the first six weeks of the final quarter of 2010, when the US central bank bought government bonds as part of the POMO, the S&P 500 rose 12 times, was flat once and fell (only slightly) twice on these days. As one-way bets go, it doesn't get much better than that.

As Jeremy Batstone-Carr, head of equity research at stockbroker Charles Stanley, succinctly pointed out in the autumn of 2010: "When Fed officials refer to 'getting the job done' what they mean is raising the price of equities. The Bernanke solution (chairman of the US Federal Reserve) is to drive the 'wealth effect', thus pushing consumption higher and spurring the economy to create jobs. Furthermore, the second round of quantitative easing is having a significant impact on liquidity, and by that we mean global liquidity." (*Investors Chronicle*, 'Fed's winter wonderland', 10 November 2010).

QE boosts equities

This affected a number of other financial markets, including the UK stock market. Mr Batstone-Carr noted at the time: "The correlation between the S&P 500 and the FTSE All-Share is incredibly close; and the long-held inverse correlation [of the US dollar] with the commodity complex has been a feature of the investment landscape for a long time, but over the past two months it has risen to a whopping 95 per cent."

It was therefore no surprise to see some of this liquidity seep into emerging markets, as investors moved cash into rapidly rising currency countries in Asia and Latin America. It was no surprise either, to see the US dollar come under pressure on news that the US central bank was dramatically increasing the supply of dollars in circulation by cranking up the printing presses with its QE2 programme.

The devaluation of the dollar proved good news for commodity prices during the period of QE2, and precious metals in particular, which are priced in dollars and so benefit from devaluation of the greenback as they become cheaper to buy in other currencies.

QE is still a gamble

The main gamble the US central bank was making was that the 'portfolio balance channel effect' – pushing money out of government bonds and into other assets – would lift risk asset prices and cause the dollar to fall, thus boosting the US economy, and essentially scaring prudence out of savers. The second gamble was that this would boost profits and wages, rather than simply prices, which would have been counter-productive.

Ultimately, the Federal Reserve's (and Bank of England's) QE programmes were aimed at driving longer-term bond yields lower. Central bankers hoped that this would alter how investors valued equities relative to fixed income; and that by driving up the value of bonds held in many investors' portfolios, it would encourage them to rebalance their assets more towards equities, in order to maintain current allocations. In effect, the UK and US central banks were trying to incentivise fund flows into the equity market, to boost household wealth and make consumers who hold shares feel better off.

Mechanics of QE

The Fed's view was that QE2 operated through portfolio choices. When the Fed buys Treasuries, it lowers yields relative to other risk assets – forcing portfolios to shift up the risk curve. That shift incorporates strong capital flows overseas – which can be seen in rising foreign exchange reserves. In turn, emerging market authorities tend to print domestic currency to buy US dollars, in order to prevent excessive currency appreciation. This then raises deposits at banks, inducing a lending boom, which is commodities intense; bullish for commodities, with knock-on effects on commodity currencies and speculative flows.

It is also worth noting what happens when QE ends, or when investors start to think it will end. When this happens, you can expect Treasury yields to rise relative to other asset classes, making them more attractive and forcing portfolios to shift back down the risk curve. This will induce capital to flow back to the US – directly boosting the US dollar – and force emerging market central banks to retire domestic currency as the dollars exit, leading to stalling bank deposit growth and stalling loan growth. This, in turn, is likely to trigger a reversal of speculative flows and could lead to credit stress among companies with weaker credit ratings.

But by April 2013, we were not there yet. The Fed was still making open-ended asset purchases of US Treasuries and mortgage-backed securities of $85bn a month, and had more than quadrupled its balance sheet to over $3.2bn in a four-and-a-half-year period (November 2008 to April 2013), through its QE1, QE2 and QE3 programmes. The Bank of England had been just as aggressive, having made £375bn of purchases of UK government securities between the start of 2009 and April 2013. As a result the UK central bank was by far the largest holder in the UK gilt market.

Implications of QE on UK equities

Equities boomed during the first two instalments of QE from the US Federal Reserve. The MSCI World index soared 39 per cent between November 2008 – when Fed chairman Ben Bernanke signalled the US central bank's intention to pursue this line of monetary policy – and March 2010 when QE1 ended. The performance of the MSCI Emerging Markets index was even better. In US dollar terms, the index doubled during that 20-month period.

It was a similar story with QE2, the start of which was signalled by Mr Bernanke in August 2010, and the programme ran until June 2011. In this 10-month period, the MSCI World index and MSCI Emerging Markets index rose by 24 per cent and 19 per cent respectively. Not surprisingly, UK equities fared well, with the FTSE 250 rising by 74 per cent during QE1 and 24 per cent while the Fed's QE2 programme was running. This was the best performing UK index, comfortably beating the returns on the FTSE 100 and SmallCap indices.

Table 17.1   QE and performance of equities

Index	QE1 (November 2008 to March 2010)	QE2 (August 2010 to June 2011*)	ECB LTRO (December 2011 to March 2012)
	Performance (%)	Performance (%)	Performance (%)
MSCI World index	39.1	24.0	12.7
MSCI Emerging Markets index	101.9	19.1	14.3
FTSE 100	36.2	16.4	9.3
FTSE 250	74.3	24.0	18.4
FTSE Small Caps	61.4	19.0	16.1
Investment trusts	2.6	2.1	1.1

*Bernanke signalled more QE in August 2010

Source: *Investors Chronicle*, 'Profit from QE', 8 August 2012

Table 17.2   Best performing FTSE 350 sectors during QE

FTSE 350 sector	QE1 (November 2008 to March 2010) Performance versus the market (%)	QE2 (August 2010 to June 2011*) Performance versus the market (%)	ECB LTRO (December 2011 to March 2012) Performance versus the market (%)
Electronic & electrical equipment	19.9	47.3	16.3
Auto & parts	73.7	43.8	5.4
Industrial metals & mining	541.1	36.4	4.0
Industrial engineering	72.5	34.0	2.1
Technology hardware & equipment	83.1	23.1	3.0
Chemicals	50.6	21.4	15.0
Forestry & paper	93.0	19.3	21.2
Personal goods	96.6	18.3	11.3
Oil equipment & services	49.6	15.4	11.2
Support services	7.6	9.0	8.6
General industrials	7.2	8.3	12.1
Software & computer services	43.1	6.7	4.8
Financial services	4.7	6.7	8.2
Real estate investment & services	16.5	6.3	3.0
Beverages	6.8	3.4	4.8
Media	12.0	3.3	1.6
Investment trusts	2.6	2.1	1.1
UK market	**43.1**	**16.4**	**10.9**

*Bernanke signalled more QE in August 2010

Source: *Investors Chronicle*, 'Profit from QE', 8 August 2012

| Table 17.3 | Worst performing FTSE 350 sectors during QE |

FTSE 350 sector	QE1 (November 2008 to March 2010) Performance versus the market (%)	QE2 (August 2010 to June 2011*) Performance versus the market (%)	ECB LTRO (December 2011 to March 2012) Performance versus the market (%)
Gas, water & multi-utilities	-28.9	-13.8	-1.3
Food retail	-5.8	-13.4	-16.1
Pharmaceuticals	-16.1	-7.8	-10.1
Mobile telecoms	-14.3	-5.8	-10.4
Food producers	-2.0	-0.4	-7.3

*Bernanke signalled more QE in August 2010

Source: *Investors Chronicle*, 'Profit from QE', 8 August 2012

Target sectors to enhance performance

The performance of the indices in western markets was impressive, but the best of the gains were made by focusing on specific sectors that can be expected to perform well while the US central bank is flooding liquidity into the global monetary system.

In a brilliant piece of research, fellow *Investors Chronicle* columnist and technical analyst, Dominic Picarda, analysed the sector performances in the UK stock market during QE1, QE2 and during the European Central Bank's (ECB) longer-term refinancing operations (LTRO). The latter programme ran between December 2011 and March 2012, and involved the ECB giving a lifeline to 589 of the region's banks, including UK banks with European operations, by providing a €1 trillion (£810bn) line of cheap three-year money (*Investors Chronicle*, 'Profit from QE', 8 August 2012).

Not surprisingly, virtually all of the biggest winners from QE were in cyclical industries with the greatest sensitivity to the wider economy, and the laggards were in sectors that were the least economically sensitive.

QE3 winners

It is also fair to say that QE3 has worked too. Although speculation was rife in the summer of 2012 that the Fed would once again turn on the printing presses, and equity markets had already rallied strongly in advance of the US central bank's official announcement on 13 September that year, the medium-term positive impact on equity markets was just the same.

In fact, although the S&P 500 had surged 11.5 per cent in the three months ahead of the Fed's announcement of QE3, this didn't stop the index rising a further 10 per cent to an all-time high in April 2013. In the UK, the gains were even more striking. The FTSE 250 rose 15 per cent in the three months prior to the Fed's announcement, as speculation mounted, and subsequently jumped a further 19 per cent in the following six months.

The five top sector winners in the UK were largely as expected in the six-month period between mid-September 2012 (when QE2 was announced by the Fed) and mid-March 2013. The FTSE 350 sectors were technology hardware (50 per cent gain); forestry and paper (40 per cent); automobiles (25 per cent); industrial engineers (25 per cent); and electronic and electrical equipment (22 per cent).

There were only two major sector winners from the QE2 programme that failed to outperform the market during QE3. These were mining (5 per cent gain) and chemicals (8 per cent gain), which performed more like the expected laggards: food retailers and utilities (both 6 per cent gain); pharmaceuticals (5 per cent gain); and mobile telecoms (3.1 per cent gain).

The relative underperformance of the FTSE 350 mining sector during QE3 is very interesting. One explanation could be that, if these massive QE programmes ultimately lead to rising inflation, as some economists believe will happen, then mining stocks may now be viewed as a relatively poor inflation hedge. That's because all the major resource giants have been undergoing multi-billion dollar capital expenditure programmes in recent years, and although a number have been shelved or reined back, it means their cost bases are much larger than previously.

In turn, the ability of miners to generate rising free cash flow in a rising inflation environment could be hindered by the massive increases in capital expenditure. We will have to wait and see whether the cumulative effects of QE do lead to rising inflation. But if the perception is that the spending plans of global miners have placed them in a worse position to ride through an environment of rising inflation, then it would certainly explain some of the underperformance of the sector during QE3.

ECB launches a bond bazooka

Financials also performed strongly during QE3, but this was mainly due to a game-changing announcement from the European Central Bank (ECB) in late summer 2012, to finally agree to launch its bond bazooka. This involved the central bank employing its massive balance sheet to purchase government bonds from the southern Mediterranean block of countries, to stop the region's debt contagion spreading any further (*Investors Chronicle*, 'Reasons to be bullish', 21 December 2012).

This policy decision, albeit belated, had bond bears running for cover and led to a dramatic fall in secondary market sovereign bond yields for both Italy and Spain. As a result, a significant amount of risk embedded in equity market valuations due to a potential break-up of the eurozone had been removed.

The resulting easing of stress in the financial sector proved a boon for life assurers which have substantial holdings in the corporate and eurozone bond markets. This sector rose 23 per cent between mid-September 2012 and mid-March 2013, and that was after having already risen over 20 per cent in the previous three months. UK banks did incredibly well too, rising by 28 per cent in the six months to mid-March 2013, as credit conditions eased.

Key lessons to learn:

■ **Fed's QE programmes are a buy signal for equities.** Periods when these programmes have been running have coincided with the best of the gains for western stock markets.

■ **Economically sensitive sectors outperform in early stages of a new Fed QE programme.** In the UK, the sectors that have performed best over QE1, QE2 and QE3 are: technology hardware; forestry and paper; automobiles; industrial engineers; and electronic and electrical equipment.

■ **Defensives underperform in early stages of a new Fed QE programme.** The sectors to avoid are: pharmaceuticals; food retailers; utilities and mobile telecoms.

■ **Expect western equity markets to struggle without the benefit of QE.** Of course, this comes with a major proviso that signs of sustainable economic growth prove elusive.

■ **Don't fight the Fed!**

18

Inflation

In the last chapter I discussed at length the ways to benefit most from quantitative easing programmes. Assuming they work, this will raise consumption and drive economies back into growth. But when that happens it is only reasonable to assume that inflation will rise too. This has obvious implications for equity markets since some sectors do well during periods of rising inflation and some should be avoided at all costs.

Fortunately I have a good idea how equities are likely to behave in such an environment, thanks to the invaluable assistance of both Credit Suisse Investment Bank and the London Business School.

Andrew Garthwaite, managing director of Credit Suisse global investment banking in London, and his global equity strategy team at the bank, considered the implications for equities in an environment where there was modest inflation, and rising inflation expectations. The research was carried out in collaboration with the London Business School (2013 Credit Suisse Global Investment Returns Yearbook, February 2013).

Good and bad inflation

Mr Garthwaite views inflation as "a good thing if it is 'demand pull' inflation. Namely, where companies have pricing power and selling prices are rising more than input prices. But bad if it is 'cost-push' inflation, when companies face higher commodity prices or wage costs rise, which in turn squeezes margins as they are unable to pass them on."

Interestingly, Credit Suisse believes that the direction of wage growth, or unit labour costs, is the best proxy for underlying inflation. That's because around two-thirds of corporate costs are from the labour market. As a result, "higher wages enable companies to pass on some of their higher costs due to the increase in consumers' disposable income."

This has implications for commodity-led inflation. That's because unless higher commodity prices are accompanied by a similar rise in wages, then the purchasing power of the consumer falls and the inflation is only short term. This is not the type of inflation companies want, because margins get squeezed as they are unable to pass on their higher input prices to consumers, whose spending power is also being squeezed by subdued wage growth.

Not surprisingly, how investors react to inflation is dependent on the extent to which it is rising. Credit Suisse found that "historically, moving from deflation to mild inflation leads to a re-rating of equities, while moving from moderate inflation to high inflation leads to a de-rating of equities. The tipping point between the two outcomes has been inflation of around 3 per cent to 4 per cent." The research was based on US data dating back to 1871.

The key issue is how real bond yields (the difference between nominal yields and the inflation rate) react to higher inflation. Mr Garthwaite explains this as follows:

■ If high inflation is a shock, and there is no deliberate effort on the part of governments or central banks to push down real bond yields, then real bond yields are likely to rise dramatically, something that has historically been very negative for financial assets.

■ Alternatively, if higher inflation is part of a deliberate policy to drive down real bond yields (known as financial repression), then rising inflation expectations lead to lower real bond yields, which should in turn re-rate financial assets.

In other words, the effect of inflation on equities is determined by a number of factors, including: the type of inflation; future inflation expectations; actual level of inflation and the impact inflation has on real bond yields.

Implications for equities

The research from Credit Suisse and the London Business School revealed that historically equities tend to de-rate when inflation falls below 2 per cent. This is a logical reaction by investors as pricing power for companies is far harder to come by in such a low inflation environment. It also explains why both the US and UK equity markets were trading on much lower earnings multiples in April 2013 than they were at their bull market peaks in October 2007; even though the S&P 500 had scaled new heights in the US, and the FTSE 100 in the UK was within a few percentage points of its previous bull market high. The intervening five-and-a-half-year period was characterised by very low inflation, or periods of recession in both the US, UK and Europe. Expectations of inflation during this time were low too, which held back the rating on these markets.

Mr Garthwaite also found that "when inflation rises above 4 per cent, equities also start to de-rate for two main reasons: first, the rise in inflation leads to a rise in real bond yields and second, the rise in inflation is often associated with economies overheating, which leads to a rise in short-term interest rates." As a result, the increase in short interest rates raises the discount rate for equities, which has negative implications for valuations. I discussed how the discount rate influences the valuation of equities in the section on interest rate cycles in Chapter 11.

An overheating economy is also bad for equities because it leads to below-trend economic growth, and falling corporate earnings at the same time that the discount rate is rising. A higher real bond yield is negative for equity market valuations, because it pushes up the discount rate and impacts the ability of indebted governments to finance their deficits.

In fact, there is a point that equities will actually perform worse than bonds. According to Credit Suisse, this is when inflation is above 8 per cent. This is understandable because "the more the inflation rate rises, the more uncertainty there is about future inflation, and the higher the real bond yield becomes".

Key lessons to learn:

- Higher real bond yield is negative for equity market ratings because it pushes up the discount rate.

- Equities start to de-rate when inflation rises above 4 per cent or falls below 2 per cent.

- Equities will perform worse than bonds when inflation rises above 8 per cent.

Good news for investors

The good news for equity market investors is that future rises in inflation are unlikely to be associated with a rise in the real bond yield.

Mr Garthwaite explains: "We believe that central banks will seek to keep nominal rates from rising through further asset purchases, and that rising inflation will be associated with a fall in the real bond yield. This is because of the need for financial repression. In the long run, governments will have to stabilize government debt to GDP and unemployment."

He has a point, saying that western governments need to "cut their debt levels and can only do so by either: improving the underlying growth rate; defaulting; tightening fiscal policy; or lowering real rates." The preferred option is "to reduce real bond yields as this reduces the amount by which fiscal policy needs to be tightened and also boosts GDP growth".

In fact Credit Suisse strategists calculate that, in order to stabilise both government debt to GDP and unemployment, the US needs to have real interest rates of minus 1.6 per cent. The required real rate is even lower in the UK. In other words, there is an incentive for both the UK and US governments, and their central banks, to adopt policies that result in nominal interest rates remaining below the inflation rate in these countries.

Equities re-rate as real bond yields fall and inflation expectations rise

If this scenario pans out it would be good for equities, because a rise in inflation expectations, associated with a decline in the real bond yield would re-rate equities. This seems a sensible assumption to make, given that Credit Suisse found that in the five years between 2008 and early 2013, "the prospective earnings multiple for the S&P 500 has been closely correlated with inflation expectations. Indeed, the single most important driver of valuations has been inflation expectations."

So if real bond yields fall in the future as inflation expectations rise, this has implications for where to invest to hedge inflation. Credit Suisse identifies the following key areas:

■ **Companies with inflation-linked pricing**. The obvious ones are utilities.

■ **Growth stocks**: The more real bond yields fall, the more growth companies benefit from a lower discount rate on their future (rising) earnings and cash flows.

■ **Real estate.** In particular, UK commercial real estate offers a record gap between the underlying property yield and the index-linked gilt yield. US, German and Japanese real estate is also among the cheapest globally, according to Credit Suisse.

■ **Gold.** Although gold stocks have performed poorly between mid-September 2012 and April 2013, and the gold price has been in a downtrend since peaking at an all-time high in September 2011, historically gold has done well in periods of negative real interest rates. That's well worth noting if real bond yields fall in the future as inflation expectations rise. Mr Garthwaite notes that in this environment "the more real bond yields fall, the more gold should rise." This is logical, as the opportunity cost of holding gold is low in a low interest rate environment, and the yellow metal has over the long run held its value when the price is adjusted for inflation.

Rising real bond yields

However, if the expectation is that real bond yields will rise, because bond yields are rising more than the inflation – this is negative for equity valuations – Mr Garthwaite suggests that investors should focus on high-dividend-yielding companies with negative working capital. Namely, businesses that are paid before they pay their creditors. In this scenario, the winners in this inflation environment are likely to be companies in three specific sectors: food, retail and telecoms.

19

How to invest like Warren Buffett

There is no question in my mind that Warren Buffett is the greatest investor of all time. The sage of Omaha, as he is widely known, enjoyed a privileged start in the finance world, as his father Howard Buffett ran a stockbroking house and encouraged his son's interest in the markets.

Moreover, having studied economics at Columbia Business School, Warren Buffett was taught by one of the greatest investors of all time, Benjamin Graham, the father of value investing, on whose works I based the criteria for my annual bargain shares portfolios in *Investors Chronicle*. If that was not enough of a head start in his investment career, Warren Buffett was fortunate enough to work with Mr Graham too. Still, Mr Buffett had to put his investment knowledge and skills into practise.

Incredible long-term gains

On this score, there is no getting away from the fact that, over almost half a century, Warren Buffett's Berkshire Hathaway investment vehicle has proved itself to be the most successful investment company of all time. In fact an investment in Berkshire Hathaway has returned an incredible 586,817 per cent increase in book value over the 48 years since its inception.

To put it another way, if you were fortunate enough to have invested $19 in just one unit of Berkshire Hathaway stock back in 1964 you would now be sitting on an investment with a book value of $114,214. That represents a compound annual growth rate of 19.7 per cent a year. And to put that into some perspective, the same investment in the S&P 500 has not even grown at half that rate, posting an annualised increase of 9.4 per cent over the same 48-year period, including dividend income. The difference between the two returns – more than 10 per cent a year – is what most fund managers struggle to achieve from their portfolios each year, let alone the excess return over the market.

Furthermore, in this winning 48-year stretch, Berkshire Hathaway has beaten the annual return on the S&P 500 benchmark in no fewer than 43 calendar years. Only twice – in 2001 and 2008 – did the book value per share of Berkshire Hathaway actually fall. But it took exceptional circumstances for that to happen: the 2000-02 bear market in the aftermath of the dot-com boom; and the financial crisis and Wall Street crash of 2008. Even then, the fall in Berkshire Hathaway's book value per unit of stock – 6.2 per cent and 9.6 per cent respectively, in those two years – hardly proved disastrous. The lost ground was fully recouped the following year in each case.

It's for this reason that I have studied the investment philosophy and techniques of Warren Buffett more than any other investor alive, or dead. In this chapter I will endeavour to show what I have learned from the greatest investor of all time. He is also one of the richest, holding shares in Berkshire Hathaway worth over $40bn.

Create a margin of safety

Warren Buffett and his right-hand man, Charlie Munger, the vice chairman of Berkshire Hathaway, have succeeded in generating these eye-watering returns because they have adhered to strict rules when assessing any potential investment.

The most important of these is to create a margin of safety in the price you are willing to pay for a company's shares, and to be patient until Mr Market is willing to offer you that price. Frankly, if you are a long-term investor then you can afford to wait months, if not years in some cases, for the market to provide you with the buying opportunity you have been waiting for, at the price you are prepared to pay. That's why Berkshire Hathaway proved itself an astute buyer in 2008 when financial markets were falling out of bed. As Warren Buffett commented in the annual report that year:

"We made purchases totalling $14.5bn in fixed-income securities issued by Wrigley, Goldman Sachs and General Electric. We very much like these commitments, which carry high current yields that in themselves, make the investments more than satisfactory. But in each of these three purchases, we also acquired a substantial equity participation as a bonus."

---

case Study 32

Margin of safety mitigates risk

The investment in Goldman Sachs in the autumn of 2008 was a classic Warren Buffett investment. The Wall Street investment bank needed to raise fresh capital, as did all US banks, on the insistence of the US bank regulator following the sub-prime mortgage crisis.

So to help meet the new capital requirements, Goldman Sachs issued $5bn of preferred shares, paying a 10 per cent annual dividend to Berkshire Hathaway in late September 2008. The company also received call warrants granting it the right to buy $5bn of Goldman Sachs common stock at $115 per share (or 43.5m shares) in the following five years.

It didn't take long for Goldman Sachs to be in a position to repay Berkshire Hathaway. In fact, the bank called in the preferred stock for redemption in April 2011, at a premium of 10 per cent over par value, plus accrued and unpaid dividends. As a result, Berkshire Hathaway earned around $1.75bn ($1.25bn in dividends plus a redemption premium of $500m) in just two-and-a-half years on its investment of $5bn, which represents a return of 35 per cent from the preferred stock alone. But importantly it still had a free carry on the equity through the 43.5m call warrants on the common stock. By March 2013, the stock in the bank was trading at $146 a share, a 27 per cent premium to the exercise price of the warrants.

In a neat bit of financial engineering, six months before the call warrants expired, Berkshire Hathaway converted the warrants into

Goldman Sachs' shares equal in value to the difference between the warrants' exercise price and the price of the shares. This transaction gave Berkshire Hathaway around 9.2m shares in Goldman Sachs, worth $1.35bn, but importantly, the company didn't have to stump up a cent for them. In effect, Berkshire Hathaway made a profit of over $3bn in only four-and-a-half years, but had a free ride for the last two years of that period.

True, no one else could follow the lead of Warren Buffett and replicate the transaction with Goldman Sachs. But you could have ridden on his coat-tails. That's because, shortly after Berkshire Hathaway's investment was made, Goldman Sachs' stock was trading as low as $53 a unit in November 2008, only to sharply recover all the lost ground by March 2009. By October 2009, one year after Berkshire Hathaway had made its investment, Goldman Sachs' shares had more than trebled in value from that low of $53 a unit in November 2008 to a high of $189.

In other words, anyone backing Warren Buffett's judgement and buying Goldman Sachs' stock at any point in that 12-month period would have made a profit on the common stock – and substantially so.

Key lessons to learn:

■ Only when he is convinced about the quality of a business does Warren Buffett consider what price he should pay. If there is no bargain on offer, he will wait patiently until some circumstance causes the stock price to fall.

■ Goldman Sachs met Berkshire Hathaway's other main investment requirements. These are:
  (a) Is the business a strong franchise with growth potential and pricing power?
  (b) Is it conservatively financed and run by managers of the highest integrity?
  (c) Does the business generate a high return on equity, and can it reinvest these earnings at continuing superior rates of return?
  (d) How much free cash will it generate over time?

■ Warren Buffett had calculated two things: first, what was an acceptable return to make on Goldman Sachs' preferred stock; and second, the probability of the bank's common stock recovering in value, above the strike price of the call warrants in the five years after Berkshire Hathaway made its investment.

■ The structure of the deal meant that Berkshire Hathaway had an option to buy Goldman Sachs' equity at less than half the level the stock was trading at only 12 months previously ($236 per unit record high in October 2007). Namely, the slump in the bank's stock price offered an opportunity for Berkshire Hathaway to take advantage of a favourable buying opportunity at a price that offered substantial potential long-term rewards.

Goldman Sachs' book value per unit of common stock was $99.30 before Berkshire Hathaway made its investment, so the exercise price of the warrants was only 16 per cent above book value, and at a 32 per cent premium to tangible book value of $87.11. Considering Goldman Sachs' had been making an annualised return on shareholders' equity of at least 20 per cent in each of the previous four financial years, then the premium was modest.

■ Warren Buffett is a long-term investor, and views sharp corrections in markets and stock prices as an opportunity to buy stock in good-quality companies at a price that will be favourable to generating long-term rewards. And because his ideal holding period is forever, he can afford to ride out volatile moves in financial markets.

This is an important point because most investors are fearful when stock markets have fallen heavily, and less inclined to buy. This short-term view, driven by the fear of accumulating short-term paper losses if the market falls further, is at odds with Warren Buffett's view that the best time to buy is when the stock market sale is on.

The key for Warren Buffett is whether the entry price is attractive enough to generate long-term gains on a holding, and not whether there is further downside in the short term. In the case of Goldman Sachs, the common stock didn't bottom out for another seven weeks after Berkshire Hathaway invested. But this didn't matter because the company was in the investment for the long term, and the implicit potential return embedded in the investment when Berkshire Hathaway made its purchase was favourable.

■ Warren Buffett does not try to call market tops or bottoms. He is more interested in the intrinsic value of a stock and a company's ability to grow. This explains why, since 1970, Berkshire Hathaway's preferred measure of value – book value per unit of stock – has grown at 19.4 per cent a year on average, which is bang in line with the 20.8 per cent annualised growth rate in the company's earnings per share.

It also explains why I view a company's ability to grow its net asset value per share over the long term as an important indicator of management's ability to create value. I highlighted this in chapter 11 with case study 24 on Sheffield-based construction and property company Henry Boot.

Think big

Within a week of the Goldman Sachs transaction, Berkshire Hathaway duplicated the deal by purchasing $3bn in preferred stock in General Electric, one of the largest US industrial companies by market value, and received call warrants to buy another $3bn in common stock at $22.25 (a 9 per cent discount to the open market price at the time) within five years. Three years later and Berkshire Hathaway sold the preferred stock back to General Electric at a 10 per cent premium, having pocketed a $300m dividend each year, but still retained the call warrants on the common stock.

In August 2011, Berkshire Hathaway invested $5bn in Bank of America's preferred stock that pays a fixed dividend of 6 per cent. The bank can buy it back at any point – for a 5 per cent premium. Berkshire also received warrants to buy 700m common shares in Bank of America (about 6.5 per cent of the company's issued share capital) at an exercise price of $7.14 a unit until 2021. By April 2013, the bank's common stock had risen by 68 per cent in value to over $12 a unit, so the call warrants were showing a paper profit of over $3bn, or more than Berkshire Hathaway's investment in the preferred stock alone.

These transactions highlight two major points:

■ In order to mitigate the risk of making a bad investment decision carry out extensive research, and create a shortlist of companies you are happy to purchase shares in at a specific price. Then wait for the market price to come to you.

■ Having waited for the chance to buy shares in a good quality company, at an attractive price, then don't be afraid to invest heavily.

Invest for the long term

Part of the reason for the incredible annualised growth rate posted by Berkshire Hathaway is down to the benefit of compounding.

Let's assume you are a buy-and-hold investor, and hold a portfolio for 10 years which grows at a rate of 20 per cent a year. Within four years, it will have doubled in value; within six years it has trebled and by the end of the tenth year it has increased by 519 per cent. That's the benefit of compounding. At the end of the tenth year you sell up and pay capital gains tax on the proceeds at 28 per cent. So an initial £10,000 investment has increased in value to £61,900, of which the tax man will take a £14,500 slice of the £51,900 gains. That leaves you with a cash sum of £47,400 after 10 years.

Alternatively, let's assume you are a short-term investor, and manage to make the same 20 per cent a year return on your capital. However, at the end of each tax year, the taxman takes his 28 per cent slice of your realised capital gains. This means that after one year, your £10,000 starting capital will have grown to £12,000 as before, but of this £560 is passed straight over to the tax man. Repeat this process over a 10-year period, and at the end of the tenth year, the £10,000 original investment has turned into a cash sum of £38,400 after all taxes are paid. That's £9,000 less than a long-term investor has made, which is a sizeable sum on a starting bank of £10,000.

Moreover, the longer the time frame, the bigger the difference in the final portfolio value of a long-term and short-tem investor. The lesson is clear: don't over-trade; investing for long-term gains pays the greatest rewards.

Don't over-leverage

Warren Buffett is never a forced seller. That's because Berkshire Hathaway uses leverage sparingly. In the business principles outlined in the company owner's manual, Warren Buffett states:

"We use debt sparingly and, when we do borrow, we attempt to structure our loans on a long-term fixed-rate basis. We will reject interesting opportunities rather than over-leverage our balance sheet. This conservatism has penalized our results but it is the only behaviour that leaves us comfortable..... The financial calculus that Charlie and I employ would never permit our trading a good night's sleep for a shot at a few extra percentage points of return."

Avoid companies diluting shareholders' interests

Berkshire Hathaway only issues stock when it receives as much in business value as it gives. This rule applies to all forms of issuance – not only mergers or public stock offerings, but stock-for-debt swaps, stock options and convertible securities as well.

So if a company is diluting its earnings per share by making an acquisition, or issuing equity for any other reason, always ask yourself how it intends to create value for shareholders in the long run.

Don't allow accounting standards to influence operating or capital-allocation decisions

When acquisition costs are similar, Berkshire Hathaway prefers to purchase $2 of earnings that are not reportable under standard accounting principles than to purchase $1 of earnings that is. Over time, the unreported earnings will be fully reflected in the intrinsic business value of the company's holdings through capital gains.

This explains why I always prefer to invest in companies with conservative accounting policies, as the hidden value in the accounts will at some point reveal itself in the future.

M&A pays

As I highlighted in chapter six, it is possible to make very attractive annualised returns by playing the merger arbitrage game. By investing after a deal has been announced, you can take advantage of the valuation difference between the market price of a share and the price the deal is likely to close at. Of course you have to factor in how long the deal will take to close, and the probability of it completing in order to ascertain whether the financial rewards warrant the risk. Warren Buffett certainly does.

Buy great companies, not great stocks

Consumer monopolies are very much Warren Buffett's bag. These are companies with substantial pricing power, partly through strong brand recognition or significant intangible, but unrecognised value. They also have predictable products, which support growing earnings and cash flow.

Berkshire Hathaway's investments in Coca-Cola and consumer products manufacturer Johnson & Johnson are prime examples of corporations with durable competitive advantages. They also pass Warren Buffett's "survival test": whether or not a company will have to change much, or at all, to survive in the future.

This also explains why Berkshire Hathaway avoids commodity-based companies. These firms are characterised by low profit margins, low returns on equity, little brand name loyalty, excess capacity within their industry and erratic profits.

"Too much of a good thing can be wonderful"

Berkshire Hathaway's "Big Four" investments are in: American Express, Coca-Cola, IBM and Wells Fargo. All had good years in 2012, enabling them to pay out a total of $1.1bn in dividends to the company out of net earnings of $3.9bn. However, in Berkshire Hathaway's 2012 annual report, Warren Buffett stated:

"The $2.8bn of earnings we do not report is every bit as valuable to us as what we record. The earnings that the four companies retain are often used for share repurchases – which enhance our share of future earnings – and also for funding business opportunities that are usually advantageous. Over time we expect substantially greater earnings from these four investees."

In fact, so convinced were they by this, Berkshire Hathaway increased its ownership interest in each company during the financial year. At the end of 2012, the Big Four investments accounted for 37.3 per cent of the company's portfolio, up from 34.9 per cent a year earlier. The lesson is clear: don't be shy of increasing a portfolio's weighting towards the winners when their potential for value creation in the future (from retained earnings), is substantial.

Investing capital

Warren Buffett believes shareholders should consider themselves as owners of a company, instead of thinking they are buying just a share of the enterprise. This has implications for the way you view a company's management and its asset allocation decisions.

In last year's annual report to Berkshire Hathaway shareholders, Mr Buffett noted that: "Management should first examine reinvestment possibilities offered by its current business – projects to become more efficient, expand territorially, extend and improve product lines or to otherwise widen the economic moat separating the company from its competitors."

The next step "is to search for acquisitions unrelated to our current businesses. Here our test is simple: Do Charlie and I think we can effect a transaction that is likely to leave our shareholders wealthier on a per-share basis than they were prior to the acquisition?"

The third use of a company's funds – stock repurchases – is deemed "sensible for a company when its shares sell at a meaningful discount to conservatively calculated intrinsic value. Indeed, disciplined repurchases are the surest way to use funds intelligently: It's hard to go wrong when you're buying dollar bills for 80¢ or less."

This is why I always consider the investment rationale when deciding whether a company is sensibly employing its retained earnings, or whether there is a better use for these funds. Ultimately, the end game is to generate the maximum rewards for shareholders.

Key lessons to learn:

■ Earnings-diluting share buy-backs will clearly not maximise shareholder value, nor will buy-backs at a price above the intrinsic value of a company's shares.

■ Value-destroying acquisitions will not either, as I have already pointed out.

■ If the business is as good as you believe it is, then there should be an opportunity to reinvest retained earnings sensibly to generate long-term returns for shareholders. However, if management is unable to do so, then you should seriously ask yourself whether you should be investing in the company in the first place.

Warren Buffett stock screen

Applying the investment principles of Warren Buffett I have come up with the following Buffett-derived large-cap stock screen for the UK equity market. It includes the following nine screens:

■ **Screen out small-cap stocks**. Focus on large-cap shares with a market value above £250m to cut out the bottom end of the market.

■ **Look for firms with high profit margins**. Avoid companies in industries where the net operating margin is below average.

■ **Avoid highly indebted companies**. Exclude all companies with net debt to equity shareholders funds above 80 per cent.

■ **Focus on firms with high earnings growth rates**. Go for companies in the top-quartile of 10-year earnings growth rates, and compare the long-term growth trends with the five-year trends. This will enable you to find out how many have seen even greater earnings growth in the past three to five years.

■ **PE ratio of less than 16**. The earnings yield (the reciprocal of the PE ratio) should be well in excess of 10-year government bond yields, and at a sustainable level. This means that, as earnings grow, the shares will at least maintain their earnings multiple and provide capital gains on the investment.

■ **Above-average return on equity (ROE)**. I would suggest a ROE of at least 12 per cent, and preferably above 15 per cent, for at least the past three years.

■ **Positive free cash flow**. Look for companies with a positive free cash flow, as the ability of a company to generate cash is a sign of its underlying profitability. A company's free cash flow is calculated by taking its operating profit and adding back depreciation and amortisation charges, and then deducting capital expenditure and changes in net working capital.

■ **Project earnings growth rates into the future**. Take the company's latest EPS figure and compound this over a 10-year period by the historic average annual earnings growth over the past 10 years. This will give an estimate of the EPS in a decade's time, assuming the company can maintain its historic EPS growth rate. Then apply the average PE ratio over the past 10 years to this forward EPS figure in order to arrive at a 'target' price in 10 years' time. The aim is to generate an annual return (excluding dividends) of at least 15 per cent a year.

■ **Dividend yields of at least 2 per cent**. The annual payout should be covered at least three times by earnings per share. Look for companies that have at least managed to grow dividends over the past five years, as rising dividends will ensure some protection against inflation.

20

Top 20 tips for successful investing

At the start of this book I outlined my top 20 rules for maximising the chances of having a successful investment outcome. In this chapter, I highlight the 20 top tips I would offer as advice to any investor.

1. Have your doubts

Never invest unless everything is right. It is easier to lose money than to make it. For instance, if a share price is weak, but the fundamentals appear strong, then ask why there is such a disparity. The time to buy is when the tide has turned and not when it is still going out; otherwise you could end up in deep water.

2. If you don't understand, don't invest

If you don't understand how a company makes its money then you will not be the only one. Moreover, if you can't get a grip on the business model and operations when times are good, then you don't stand a chance when trading goes into reverse. There are enough potential investment opportunities out there to have the luxury of walking away from the ones you simply don't understand, no matter how big the hype is.

3. Set buy limits

Patience is a virtue. Having researched a company and made the decision to invest, be disciplined when it comes to investing and always set a limit on the price you are willing to pay. The investment case may be attractive at one level, but potential future returns rapidly diminish if the price has run away by the time you come to buy. So only invest when the share price is in line with your pre-set limits. Otherwise move on.

However, if you are lucky enough to get in on the ground floor, then be patient and allow enough time for others to see the merits of the investment case you had the foresight to spot first.

4. The trend is your friend

In a bull market the whole point is to be long. Not investing and waiting on the sidelines is a position in itself. Buy into strength – if a trend is strong then use minor corrections to buy into that trend. Remember the trend is meant to be your friend, so use it. The final stages of a bull run have a tendency to generate easy gains as latecomers come to the party, so ride your profits.

5. Don't be greedy

When markets are buoyant it is all too easy to get carried away. Some investors get emotionally attached to a company, which is a fatal mistake. Therefore, it is a good discipline to set target prices before you invest in any company. Even if you don't bank all the gains when the target price is hit, there is no harm in top-slicing holdings to turn paper profits into real ones.

6. Timing the exit

There comes a point when profits must be taken no matter how much money an investment has made for you, or how great the business is. Ultimately, this is when the risk-reward ratio has shifted to such an extent that the upside potential of further capital appreciation is far outweighed by the possible downside risk of capital loss.

Remember that the stock market has a tendency to overreact, and that share valuations are just as likely to overshoot as undershoot fair value. The difficulty for investors is when to call this precise point. So it's not just a case of determining whether the shares have hit a fair value, based on fundamental equity analysis, you need to know whether the technical indicators are flashing a warning signal that the rally is coming to an end.

7. Use trailing stop-losses

The mental energy expended watching a company's share price fall far outweighs the euphoria, or feel-good factor, of seeing it rise. That's why trailing stop-loss systems, which adjust the stop-loss upwards as a company's share price rises are important, as they allow profits to run and losses to be contained before all the paper gains made on a holding disappear. So if a share price falls through a trailing stop-loss the shares are sold and you move on. It's as simple as that.

8. Manage risk

Capital preservation is key in investing, so it pays to take pre-emptive action before paper losses run away.

For instance, if a holding falls in value by 10 per cent and the loss is crystallised at that point, this means that the cash put into the next investment needs to rise by 11 per cent to make good the damage. However, by the time the loss hits 20 per cent, the next investment will need to rise by 25 per cent to recoup the loss.

It gets worse the further losses escalate. That's because by the time a shareholding has lost 40 per cent of its value, and assuming you sell at this point, the next investment would need to rise by 66 per cent to make good that loss. It really doesn't bear thinking about if a holding loses half its value. In this scenario, your next investment would need to double in value to bring the position back to break-even.

9. A profit warning is seldom a one-off

The advice here is simple: when a company warns of a profit shortfall, it is seldom a one-off occurrence. So investors wishing to avoid being hit a second time should seriously think about getting out at the first warning.

10. Avoid high levels of leverage

Leverage works both ways. It can accentuate returns to the upside in spectacular fashion, but it can also lead to crippling losses when things go wrong.

To demonstrate this, consider the example of an investor who funds 25 per cent of an equity portfolio through debt and 75 per cent through cash. This means that if the market crashes 25 per cent, then once the borrowings are repaid, the investor's investment capital will have fallen by a third in value.

The sums are even scarier if the equity portfolio is geared up further still, and the level of debt matches the investor's cash investment. In this scenario, the investor loses half the original investment if the market crashes 25 per cent.

The message is clear: avoid high levels of leverage on equity investments.

11. Don't over-trade

The best investment returns are made by not just investing for the long term, but by not trading too much in the process. That's because the more you trade, the greater the chance your judgement will fail at some point. Losses could then quickly escalate and wipe out all the prior banked gains.

It is far better to buy only a small number of new shareholdings each year, assuming you have strong conviction behind each one, rather than trying to make the same total return by trading in and out of the market. In any case, the more you trade the greater the proportion of your return is being eaten away through dealing costs.

12. Assess your losers

It is important to find out why an investment has gone wrong. This not only means acknowledging the error of judgment to avoid repeating the same bad call in the future, but you also need to analyse the specific reasons why you invested unsuccessfully. The psychology of investing is as important as investing itself.

13. Don't be a gambler

The mind plays games, especially after heavy losses have been racked up. So avoid at all costs the temptation to try to recoup your money immediately. That is the mistake compulsive gamblers make. The urge can be difficult to resist, but reassess your investment strategy and ascertain why the investment failed.

14. No free lunch

If it sounds too good to be true, then it probably is. If making money from financial markets were so easy then the majority of fund managers would not underperform the indices they aim to beat. Free lunches rarely, if ever, exist.

15. Learn from the masters

The outliers of the finance world are the small group of investment minds that have managed to beat markets consistently over the long run. Anthony Bolton, who ran Fidelity Special Situations between 1979 and 2007, was one such guru having posted an annualised return of 19.5 per cent over the 28-year period, six percentage points better than the market.

Ben Graham, Philip Fisher and Warren Buffett are the other three investment managers I have tried to learn from. Berkshire Hathaway, the investment vehicle of Mr Buffett, has posted a 19.7 per cent compound annual gain in the book value per share of the company in the period between 1965 and 2012. This represents a 10.3 per cent annual outperformance of the S&P 500.

Investors able to generate such incredible long-term returns are well worth learning from.

16. The ultimate test for long-term returns

The ability of a company to generate long-term returns for shareholders will show up in its net asset value per share. This irons out changes in the capital structure resulting from share issues, and factors in the payment of dividends out of retained earnings. Dividend paying companies that can grow their book value per share in high single digits each year over the long run, are far more likely to reward shareholders with double-digit annual returns. If there is one test for value creation, then this is it.

17. Don't over-rely on earnings estimates

Avoid falling into the trap of relying too heavily on brokers' notes, and only use profit forecasts as a guide as part of your own analysis process. Analysts are only human, and are just as capable of being overly optimistic about a company's prospects as any other investor. History has shown that earnings estimates are far more likely to be reined back than upgraded, so overdependence on the profit numbers, especially where valuations offer little margin for error, is a dangerous game to play.

18. Know who analysts work for

Make sure you know whom the broker represents by differentiating between the house broker, buy side and sell side analysts. The house broker is employed by the company to advise it on corporate finance activities. These include raising equity and debt finance and evaluating possible takeover targets.

Moreover, the ability of analysts to offer independent advice can be hindered by the investment bank's corporate finance department; especially when dealmakers are tendering for merger and acquisition business. This is why a house broker will never advise selling shares in a client unless he wants to lose that company's business, and probably his job, too.

It also explains why house brokers maintain buy recommendations on shares even when the prices have hit their target prices. Bear in mind that over 90 per cent of all broker recommendations are buys in bull markets and not far off that level even in bear markets. A sure-fire way to the poor house is to take all recommendations at face value.

19. Be careful with peer-group comparisons

When a price target or valuation is justified on the basis of peer group comparisons, tread carefully. There are several other factors that influence whether a premium rating or discount to peers is justified.

These include a company's ability to generate economic profits (a measure of a company's financial performance based on the residual wealth created for shareholders after deducting the cost of capital from operating profit); return on equity and capital employed relative to cost of capital; free cash flow generation; and dividend policy (progressive or otherwise).

Peer group comparisons may indicate that on paper, a company appears undervalued, but that's not to say that the comparative is overvalued.

20. Keep an open mind

The eminent scientist and investor Alexander Graham Bell once said: "When one door closes, another door opens; but we often look so long and regretfully upon the closed door that we don't see the ones which are open for us." In a nutshell, that's what investing in equities is all about: keep an open mind and look out for the next opportunity. Good luck to you all.

References

Baron, John (2013) 'Japan: A once-in-a-lifetime opportunity', *Investors Chronicle*, 7 February.

Dillow, Chris (2005) 'Make 34 per cent from four phone calls', *Investors Chronicle*, 8 July.

Dillow, Chris (2006) 'Five seasonal trading strategies', *Investors Chronicle*, 15 December.

Dillow, Chris (2007) 'Make 26 per cent the easy way', *Investors Chronicle*, 1 June.

Dillow, Chris (2010) 'Sell in May, watch your profits slip away', *Investors Chronicle*, 26 April.

Dillow, Chris (2010) 'Pumpkins, chickens and volatility', *Investors Chronicle*, 26 October.

Dillow, Chris (2012) 'Why not invest seasonally', *Investors Chronicle*, 27 April.

Dimson, Elroy and Marsh, Paul and Staunton, Mike (2013), 'Credit Suisse Global Investment Returns Yearbook and Sourcebook', Credit Suisse Research Institute and London Business School, 5 February

Garthwaite, Andrew (2013) 'Credit Suisse Global Investment Returns Yearbook and Sourcebook', Credit Suisse Research Institute and London Business School, 5 February

Investors Chronicle (2005) 'How to screen for contrarian shares', *Investors Chronicle*, 26 August.

Numis (2013), 'Spectacular performance in 2012 from small- and mid-cap UK companies', Numis Smaller Companies Index Annual Review 2013, 16 January

Picarda, Dominic (2012) 'Profit from QE', *Investors Chronicle*, 8 August.

Thompson, Simon (2001) 'Golden rules: There's more to winning with shares', *Investors Chronicle*, 9 November.

Thompson, Simon (2005) 'Stock market mastermind', *Investors Chronicle*, 22 July.

Thompson, Simon (2006) 'How to bank a fortune', *Investors Chronicle, 23 June.*

Thompson, Simon (2009) 'Merger arbitrage', *Investors Chronicle*, 30 April.

Thompson, Simon (2009) 'An investment to retire on', *Investors Chronicle*, 20 June.

Thompson, Simon (2009) 'Investing in an Ideal World', *Investors Chronicle*, 12 October.

Thompson, Simon (2010) 'Luxury at a bargain price', *Investors Chronicle*, 8 February.

Thompson, Simon (2010) 'Bargain shares', *Investors Chronicle*, 12 February.

Thompson, Simon (2010) 'Bargain shares 2009 update', *Investors Chronicle*, 12 February.

Thompson, Simon (2010) 'Hot property', *Investors Chronicle*, 4 October.

Thompson, Simon (2010) 'Fed's winter wonderland', *Investors Chronicle*, 10 November.

Thompson, Simon (2011) 'Queuebusters', *Investors Chronicle*, 17 January.

Thompson, Simon (2011) 'Bargain shares', *Investors Chronicle*, 8 February.

Thompson, Simon (2011) 'Capital returns', *Investors Chronicle*, 14 February.

Thompson, Simon (2011) 'Amber Alert', *Investors Chronicle*, 10 May.

Thompson, Simon (2011) 'A level playing field', *Investors Chronicle*, 16 May.

Thompson, Simon (2012) 'Bargain shares', *Investors Chronicle*, 10 February.

Thompson, Simon (2012) 'A small-cap trading play', *Investors Chronicle*, 12 February.

Thompson, Simon (2012) 'Dressed for success', *Investors Chronicle*, 20 February.

Thompson, Simon (2012) 'Supreme value stocks, *Investors Chronicle*, 30 April.

Thompson, Simon (2012) 'Time to capitalise on LMS Capital', *Investors Chronicle*, 25 June.

Thompson, Simon (2012) 'Spark for a rerating', *Investors Chronicle*, 10 July.

Thompson, Simon (2012) 'Vertu shares priced to motor', *Investors Chronicle*, 9 August.

Thompson, Simon (2012) 'Gold winning performance', *Investors Chronicle*, 23 October.

Thompson, Simon (2012) 'Hyper value buy', *Investors Chronicle*, 26 October.

Thompson, Simon (2012) 'A stamp of authority', *Investors Chronicle*, 5 November.

Thompson, Simon (2012) 'Rerating beckons', *Investors Chronicle*, 12 November.

Thompson, Simon (2012) 'Foundations for a rally', *Investors Chronicle*, 12 December.

Thompson, Simon (2012) 'Reasons to be bullish', *Investors Chronicle*, 21 December

Thompson, Simon (2012) 'Rampant bargain shares', *Investors Chronicle*, 31 December.

Thompson, Simon (2013) 'Stock-picking marvels', *Investors Chronicle*, 16 January.

Thompson, Simon (2013) 'Lessons to learn', *Investors Chronicle*, 23 January.

Thompson, Simon (2013) 'Time to play Russian roulette', *Investors Chronicle*, 4 February.

Thompson, Simon (2013) 'Bargain shares 2012 update', *Investors Chronicle*, 8 February.

Thompson, Simon (2013) 'Bargain shares for 2013', *Investors Chronicle*, 8 February.

Thompson, Simon (2013) 'A share ready to hit the jackpot', *Investors Chronicle*, 11 February.

Thompson, Simon (2013) 'Chart break-out for solid income play', *Investors Chronicle*, 12 February.

Thompson, Simon (2013) 'From Russia with profit', *Investors Chronicle*, 25 February.

Thompson, Simon (2013) 'Solid income buy', *Investors Chronicle*, 25 February.

Thompson, Simon (2013) 'A major buy signal beckons', *Investors Chronicle*, 11 March.

Thompson, Simon (2013) 'Full house', *Investors Chronicle*, 25 March.

Index

Notes